YORK NOTES

MACBETH

WILLIAM SHAKESPEARE

NOTES BY JAMES SALE

 Longman   York Press

YORK PRESS
322 Old Brompton Road, London SW5 9JH

PEARSON EDUCATION LIMITED
Edinburgh Gate, Harlow,
Essex CM20 2JE, United Kingdom
Associated companies, branches and representatives throughout the world

First published 1997
This new and fully revised edition first published 2002

10 9 8 7 6 5 4 3 2 1

ISBN 0–582–50591 7

Designed by Michelle Cannatella
Illustrations on pages 16, 27, 39, 44, 58, 67, 68, 70, 71, 72 by Gerry Grace
Illustrations on pages 11, 12–13, 23, 28, 38, 46, 48, 51, 55, 63 by Linda E. Sale
Phototypeset by Gem Graphics, Trenance, Mawgan Porth, Cornwall
Colour reproduction and film output by Spectrum Colour
Produced by Addison Wesley Longman China Limited, Hong Kong

CONTENTS

PREFACE

York Notes are designed to give you a broader perspective on works of literature studied at GCSE and equivalent levels. With examination requirements changing in the twenty-first century, we have made a number of significant changes to this new series. We continue to help students to reach their own interpretations of the text but York Notes now have important extra-value new features.

You will discover that York Notes are genuinely interactive. The new **Checkpoint** features make sure that you can test your knowledge and broaden your understanding. You will also be directed to excellent websites, books and films where you can follow up ideas for yourself.

The **Resources** section has been updated and an entirely new section has been devoted to how to improve your grade. Careful reading and application of the principles laid out in the Resources section guarantee improved performance.

The **Detailed summaries** include an easy-to-follow skeleton structure of the story-line, while the section on **Language and style** has been extended to offer an in-depth discussion of the writer's techniques.

The Contents page shows the structure of this study guide. However, there is no need to read from the beginning to the end as you would with a novel, play or poem. Use the Notes in the way that suits you. Our aim is to help you with your understanding of the work, not to dictate how you should learn.

Our authors are practising English teachers and examiners who have used their experience to offer a whole range of **Examiner's secrets** – useful hints to encourage exam success.

The General Editor of this series is John Polley, Senior GCSE Examiner and former Head of English at Harrow Way Community School, Andover.

The author of these Notes is James Sale. James is an experienced teacher who has specialised in making Shakespeare accessible to students.

The text used in these Notes is The New Penguin Shakespeare, revised edition, 1993.

PART ONE

INTRODUCTION

HOW TO STUDY A PLAY

Though it may seem obvious, remember that a play is written to be performed before an audience. Ideally, you should see the play live on stage. A film or video recording is next best, though neither can capture the enjoyment of being in a theatre and realising that your reactions are part of the performance.

There are six aspects of a play:

❶ THE PLOT: a play is a story whose events are carefully organised by the playwright in order to show how a situation can be worked out

❷ THE CHARACTERS: these are the people who have to face this situation. Since they are human they can be good or bad, clever or stupid, likeable or detestable, etc. They may change too!

❸ THE THEMES: these are the underlying messages of the play, e.g. jealousy can cause the worst of crimes; ambition can bring the mightiest low

❹ THE SETTING: this concerns the time and place that the author has chosen for the play

❺ THE LANGUAGE: the writer uses a certain style of expression to convey the characters and ideas

❻ STAGING AND PERFORMANCE: the type of stage, the lighting, the sound effects, the costumes, the acting styles and delivery must all be decided

Work out the choices the dramatist has made in the first four areas, and consider how a director might balance these choices to create a live performance.

The purpose of these York Notes is to help you understand what the play is about and to enable you to make your own interpretation. Do not expect the study of a play to be neat and easy: plays are chosen for examination purposes, not written for them!

 DID YOU KNOW?

Diana Wynyard, playing Lady Macbeth in 1948, said she did not believe in the play's bad luck. On the first night of her performance she slipped from the rostrum and fell fifteen feet!

AUTHOR – LIFE AND WORKS

1564 William Shakespeare is baptised on 26 April in Stratford-on-Avon, Warwickshire

1582 Marries Anne Hathaway

1583 Birth of daughter, Susanna

1585 Birth of twins, Hamnet and Judith

1590–93 Early published works and poems written when theatres are closed by the Plague

1594 Joins Lord Chamberlain's Men (from 1603 named the King's Men) as actor and playwright

1595 *Romeo and Juliet* first performed

1595–99 Writes the history plays and comedies

1597 Shakespeare bought New Place, the second biggest house in Stratford

1599 Moves to newly-opened Globe Theatre, writes *Twelfth Night*

1599–1608 Writes his greatest plays, including *Macbeth*, *King Lear* and *Hamlet*

1608–13 Takes over the lease of Blackfriars Theatre and writes final plays, the romances, ending with *The Tempest*

1609 Shakespeare's sonnets published

Globe Theatre burns down 29 June, during performance of *Henry VIII*

1616 Shakespeare dies, 23 April, and is buried in Stratford

1623 First Folio of Shakespeare's plays published

CONTEXT

1558 Elizabeth I becomes Queen of England

1568 Mary Queen of Scots is imprisoned for life

1577–80 Sir Francis Drake becomes the first to circumnavigate the world

1587 Mary Queen of Scots is executed

1588 Defeat of the Spanish Armada

1591 Tea is first drunk in England

1593–94 Outbreak of the Plague in London, closing theatres and killing as many as 5,000, according to some sources

1594 Queen Elizabeth spends Christmas at Greenwich and is entertained by leading theatre company of her day, headed by James Burbage, William Kempe and Shakespeare

1595 Walter Raleigh sails to Guiana

1599 Oliver Cromwell is born

1603 Elizabeth I dies on 24 March; James I, son of Mary, succeeds to throne of England

1604 Peace treaty signed with Spain

1605 The Gunpowder Plot

1611 The Bible is translated into the Authorised (King James) Version

1614 Fire sweeps through Stratford but New Place is spared

1618 Thirty Years War begins

SETTING AND BACKGROUND

SHAKESPEARE'S BACKGROUND

Born in Stratford upon Avon in 1564, William Shakespeare died there almost exactly fifty-two years later, in 1616. During those fifty-two years he created at least thirty-seven plays and possibly had a hand in others. He was also to write several poems, including his famous Sonnets.

He lived in an age when printing was commonplace, yet most of his works were published either after his death or without his authority. The lives of great people were increasingly being written about, yet precious little comment on Shakespeare survives from those years. As we will see, this makes *Macbeth* the more striking: we know that this play was written for a particular King at a particular moment of history. Therefore, in studying *Macbeth* we have some extra information. This, perhaps, enables us to find some greater insight into the art and mind of William Shakespeare.

CONTEXT

Macbeth was written sometime between 1603 and 1606. This coincides with the accession of James the Sixth of Scotland to the English throne, as James the First of England, in 1603. The play was certainly written with James primarily in mind and there is a story that he 'was pleas'd with his own Hand to write an amicable letter to Mr Shakespeare'. Whether he wrote the letter to Shakespeare or not, the play certainly shows James is his focus in a number of ways.

- First, it pays homage to the interests and expertise of James: its fascination with the supernatural courts his attention: witchcraft (Act I Scene 1, Act I Scene 3 and Act IV Scene 1), apparitions and ghosts (Act II Scene 1 and Act III Scene 4) and the King's Evil (Act IV Scene 3) were areas of great concern to James. He had even written a book, *Demonology*, on the subject.

- Second, it compliments James by making his ancestor, Banquo, a hero in the play. As Duncan puts it: 'Noble Banquo, / Thou hast no less deserved' (I.4.30–1). Yet despite also receiving supernatural

DID YOU KNOW?

Many writers throughout history have composed their works for Kings, Queens or rich or important persons. This is called patronage.

DID YOU KNOW?

The Divine Right of Kings meant that because God appointed the king, the king was not answerable to the people or to Parliament.

solicitation, he – unlike Macbeth – does not fall into evil. Furthermore, as Macbeth admits, Banquo's is the greater spirit: 'under him / My genius is rebuked' (III.1.54–5). This is dramatically apt – but in point of fact, Banquo historically was an accomplice in the murder of Duncan. A reminder of this, presumably, would not have pleased James.

- Third, the play explores the issue of kingship and loyalty. These were of profound importance to James, who early in life had survived an assassination attempt. Moreover, his father, Lord Darnley, had been murdered and his mother, Mary Queen of Scots, had been executed as a traitor. Thus, questions of the role of the monarch and the duties of their subjects towards them, were ever in the forefront of his mind. Within the space of forty years, it was James's son, Charles the First, whose insistence upon the Divine Right of Kings led to the English Civil War and his own downfall and death.

- Fourth, the play is intimately related to the topical events of the Gunpowder Plot of 1605 and the subsequent trials of its conspirators. This failed coup was sensational in a number of ways – the sheer audacity of blowing up Parliament amazed the country, as did the scale of the treachery involved. Shakespeare himself almost certainly knew some of the conspirators. Some were from Shakespeare's home county, Warwickshire. The discovery of the plot, late in the day, seemed miraculous – James thought it so. And the trial itself cast Catholicism in a bad light: Father Garnett defended 'equivocation', which meant that lies under oath were morally justified. Shakespeare picks up this theme in the play: Banquo talks of the 'truths' which betray us (I.3.123), and the Porter debates the equivocator who 'could not equivocate to heaven' (II.3.10–11). This is related to the wider theme of appearances. It was Lady Macbeth who advises Macbeth to 'look like the innocent flower, / But be the serpent under't' (I.5.63–4).

SUCCESSION AND ORDER

It should be clear from the points concerning James the First that the world Shakespeare lived in was very different from today's. Of paramount importance was the political issue of succession and order. Shakespeare was born during the reign of Queen Elizabeth the First. Although Elizabeth would rule long and prosperously, this did not disguise the fact that there was an immense potential for subversion throughout her reign: the Tudor dynasty had successfully healed the wounds caused by the civil war known as the War of the Roses. However, it was not long after England had recovered from this dreadful event that Henry the Eighth, Elizabeth's father, renounced the Roman Catholic faith and established the Church of England. This created a double problem for national unity. First, one of Henry's children, Mary, succeeded to the throne and forcibly re-established the Catholic faith. On Mary's death, her half sister, Elizabeth succeeded and reasserted the Protestant faith – the issue of belief, therefore, became one which threatened to divide the country once more. Second, alongside it, 'true' Catholic countries like Spain became the enemies of England – and until the defeat of the Spanish Armada in 1588 there was a real danger of invasion by Spain to restore Catholicism. The Gunpowder Plot itself was a last desperate gamble by the Catholics to reassert, as they saw it, the 'true' faith.

Elizabeth remained the 'Virgin' Queen throughout her reign, which meant she had no natural successor. This created further instability – the Essex rising of 1601 in which Shakespeare's friend and patron, the Earl of Southampton was involved and imprisoned as a result, was a symptom of the need for political certainty – Elizabeth herself did not name her successor till she actually came to her death-bed.

? DID YOU KNOW?
Shakespeare dedicated two poems to the Earl of Southampton, and many think he is also featured in Shakespeare's Sonnets.

The country, therefore, knew only too well the dire implications of insurrection and anarchy – such events were only too recent in their mind. And they had to be avoided in future – hence the importance of order, degree and loyalty. This order – hierarchy, even – had not only political but religious backing: God had created a world of order. We might now call it a 'pecking order'. We see a reference to it at Macbeth's feast. He invites his assembled guests to sit down: 'You know your own degrees' (III.4.1). Where one sits is determined by rank. By divine appointment, the King ruled over men and to violate or seek to violate this situation was against God's Will thereby producing 'unnatural' results. Thus, the unnatural killing of Duncan is accompanied by, amongst other things, 'A falcon [a sovereign bird] towering in her pride of place / Was by a mousing owl [an inferior bird] hawked at and killed [so, an unnatural event]' (II.4.12–13).

WITCHCRAFT

CHECK THE FILM

Ken Hughes' version of *Macbeth*, called *Joe Macbeth* (1956) is unusual – the play is set in gangland America of the 1930s.

This question of 'unnaturalness' links thematically to the other striking aspect of *Macbeth*'s plot and staging: witchcraft. We must remember that England was not the industrial, scientific and urban society it largely is now. Belief in witchcraft and demonology was widespread. The objection to it – and in 1604 its practice became punishable by death – was precisely that it attempted to subvert God's natural order. We see this clearly in the Weird Sisters: females who have beards (I.3.45) and who in their spells invoke a 'birth-strangled babe / Ditch-delivered by a drab' (IV.1.30–1). They substitute death at the point of birth, and their major achievement is leading Macbeth (and many others) to destruction. Two key points for us are: how far do we see the supernatural in the play as psychological, and how far are the manifestations 'real'? The interpretation of these points is crucial for staging the play.

Now take a break!

Scottish Doctor Physician attending Lady Macbeth whom he finds incurable

English Doctor Physician attending Edward the Confessor whom he notes has the healing gift

Old Man Wisely comments on the action to Rosse.

Siward & Young Siward General of the English forces & his son who is killed in combat by Macbeth

Fleance Son of Banquo Escapes assassination attempt of Macbeth

Porter Doorkeeper at Macbeth's castle Notes he's in 'hell'

Three Witches Supernatural Creatures that prophecies draw out the evil within Macbeth

Hecate Leader of the witches

Lenox, Menteth Angus, Cathness Scottish Noblemen

Macduff Thane of Fife Nemesis/avenger to Macbeth 'not born of woman'

Lady Macduff Loyal wife of Macduff Murdered by Macbeth

Rosse Scottish nobleman wams Lady Macduff

Lady Macbeth Ambitious wife of Macbeth Commits Suicide

Banquo Friend/victim of Macbeth Father of Fleance who is destined to be king

Donalbain Brother of Malcolm Flees to Ireland

Macbeth Thane of Glamis First cousin to Duncan traitor

Duncan King of Scotland Father of Malcolm & Donalbain

Malcolm Son of Duncan Prince of Cumberland King after Macbeth

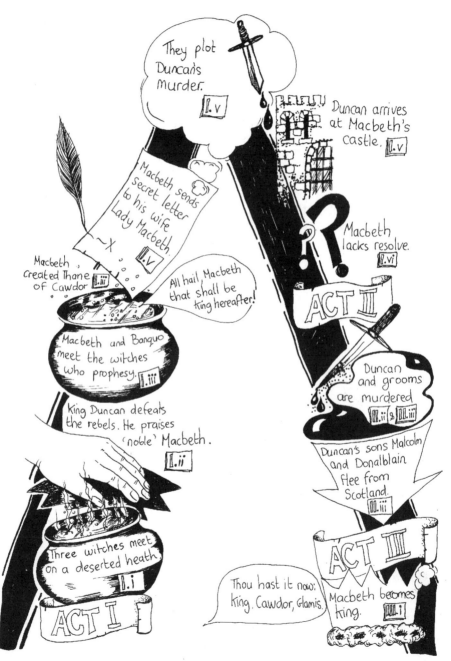

PART TWO

SUMMARIES

GENERAL SUMMARY

ACT I: PLANS AGAINST KING DUNCAN

Three witches meet in a storm and plan to encounter Macbeth. King Duncan is told how brave Macbeth and Banquo have defeated the rebels. He grants Macbeth the title Thane of Cawdor. The three witches inform Macbeth he will be Thane of Cawdor and King of Scotland. They tell Banquo his descendants will be kings. After Macbeth is officially informed that he has become the Thane of Cawdor, he reveals his hopes for the crown. Lady Macbeth, learning what has happened, shares Macbeth's ambition. She calls on spirits to give her the strength to undertake the murder of Duncan. When Macbeth arrives she insists on planning the murder. Shortly, Duncan arrives at Macbeth's castle where he is welcomed.

ACT II: ACTION AGAINST KING DUNCAN

CHECK THE NET

Look at **www. englishresources. co.uk/workunits/ ks4/shakespeare** for a useful essay on the development of Macbeth's character in Act I.

Macbeth wavers in his resolve to kill Duncan. But his wife cajoles him. After murdering Duncan, he returns to Lady Macbeth in a distraught state. She reproaches him. Lady Macbeth goes and smears the drugged and sleeping guards with the blood and guilt. They retire to bed to pretend innocence. Macduff and Lennox arrive to wake Duncan. Macduff finds Duncan murdered and the alarm is sounded. Macbeth slays the guards in fury. Macduff challenges Macbeth's action in killing the guards. As Macbeth justifies his actions, Lady Macbeth faints. In the ensuing confusion, Malcolm and Donalbain, for fear of their lives, slip away. Ross and an Old Man discuss how unnatural these events have been. Macbeth succeeds to the throne. Macduff will not attend Macbeth's coronation.

ACT III: REIGN OF KING MACBETH

Banquo suspects Macbeth. Macbeth, however, appears friendly and invites him as chief guest to his feast. Macbeth entertains two murderers whom he instructs to assassinate Banquo and his son, Fleance. Lady Macbeth is not involved. She attempts to lighten Macbeth's mood – they are both restless and sleepless. Three murderers kill Banquo but Fleance escapes. During the feast Macbeth twice sees the ghost of Banquo focusing on him. Only the quick thinking of Lady Macbeth saves Macbeth from blurting out his guilt. Later, Macbeth recovers himself and reveals he intends to act against Macduff and visit the three witches. The goddess of witchcraft, Hecate, bids the three witches properly prepare for Macbeth's visit. Suspicions against Macbeth grow. Meanwhile, Macduff has fled to Malcolm at the English court.

ACT IV: PLANS AGAINST KING MACBETH

Macbeth visits the witches and also meets their masters. He discovers that he should fear Macduff, but that nobody born of a woman can harm him. He also learns that he will reign until Birnan Wood comes to Dunsinane. To his annoyance, the prophecy relating to Banquo's offspring is confirmed. After leaving them, Macbeth finds Macduff is fled. He orders the destruction of Macduff's whole family. Ross warns Lady Macduff, but it is too late: she and her son are murdered. In England, Malcolm tests the loyalty of Macduff. Ross arrives and informs Macduff of the slaughter of his family. Malcolm informs Macduff that England will provide an army under Seyward to defeat Macbeth. Macduff vows personally to kill Macbeth.

ACT V: ACTION AGAINST KING MACBETH

Lady Macbeth is now ill: sleepwalking and talking in her sleep. Her doctor and gentlewoman realise the implications of the guilty things she is saying, but are unable to cure her. The English army marches on Macbeth who fortifies his castle at Dunsinane and prepares for a siege. Malcolm orders the boughs of trees to be cut down and used as camouflage – hence anticipating the prophecy. Macbeth hears a scream and learns his wife has died – apparently by suicide. He is unconcerned. His life appears to lack any meaning. However, he is enraged by the next message he receives: Birnan Wood is coming to Dunsinane. He abandons his siege plan and goes out fighting. His army is losing but nobody seems able to kill Macbeth. Macbeth defeats Seyward's son in combat. Then he meets Macduff. They fight, but upon learning that Macduff is not born of a woman – he was born by Caesarean operation – he loses his courage and refuses to continue. Macduff baits him and they engage to the death – Macbeth is killed. Macduff produces the head of Macbeth for Malcolm and hails him King of Scotland. Malcolm invites all to attend his coronation at Scone.

DID YOU KNOW?

Macbeth is considered to be one of the four great tragic masterpieces that Shakespeare wrote. The other three are *King Lear, Othello,* and *Antony and Cleopatra*.

DID YOU KNOW?

There is symmetry in the five-Act structure: activities in Acts I and II parallel those in Acts IV and V.

DETAILED SUMMARIES

SCENE 1 – Meeting the witches

CHECK THE FILM
The Exorcist (1973) suggests witchcraft is 'real' and still relevant today.

❶ Three witches meet and prepare to entice Macbeth to evil.

In the middle of a storm three witches (or 'Weird Sisters') assemble. Their riddling rhymes indicate that shortly they intend to meet Macbeth.

The witches are ambiguous creatures – perhaps not even human. To form a full picture you will need to study their appearances in Act I Scene 3 and Act IV Scene 1. They create a sense of mystery: they will meet 'When the battle's lost and won' (line 4), which seems a contradiction.

CHECKPOINT 1
How do the witches interest us at the beginning of the play?

The fact that they are evil is shown in their final **couplet**. According to them, 'Fair is foul, and foul is fair' (line 9). This means: good is bad and bad is good. The witches are violating God's natural order.

SCENE 2 – Macbeth and Banquo's bravery

1 A sergeant informs Duncan of the rebels' defeat.

2 Macbeth and Banquo have displayed outstanding bravery in the fight.

3 Macbeth is made Thane of Cawdor as a reward.

We switch from the shadowy world of witches to the physical world of battle.

King Duncan receives news from a wounded Captain that the battle against the traitor Macdonwald and his army was evenly balanced until Macbeth and Banquo in acts of outstanding courage and ferocity destroyed him and his troops. But as this occurs, reinforcements from the King of Norway and the traitor, the Thane of Cawdor, counterattack Macbeth and Banquo. However, these two are not at all dismayed; but as the Captain is taken away to tend his wounds, the outcome is still unsure. The Thane of Ross arrives to report that, through the fighting spirit of Macbeth, Duncan's army has won a great victory. Duncan declares that the traitor Thane of Cawdor is to be executed and Macbeth is to receive his title and estates as a reward.

Who is Macbeth?

We have not yet met Macbeth. The witches mention him earlier. Now the Captain and Ross do. Whilst the battle is primitive and bloody, yet their descriptions emphasise an heroic, even 'epic' quality about the proceedings, especially Macbeth's part in them. This is shown in the **personifications** – 'Disdaining fortune' (line 17), 'valour's minion' (line 19), 'Bellona's bridegroom' (line 56) – and references: 'memorize another Golgotha' (line 41). Duncan himself generously praises Macbeth, and the final **epithet** he gives is 'noble' (line 70).

CHECKPOINT 2

What impressions do you form of Macbeth from the comments about him so far?

GLOSSARY

Disdaining fortune unafraid of his own safety

Bellona's bridegroom Macbeth – described as a fit husband for the Roman goddess of war, Bellona

memorize another Golgotha create an event as bloody and memorable as when Christ suffered

An important distinction

The use of irony – more specifically, dramatic irony – is
particularly important. This play explores the subtle distinctions
between what appears to be so and what actually is. A good
example is Duncan's comment that the Thane of Cawdor shall no
more deceive him.

SCENE 3 The witches meet Macbeth and Banquo

❶ The witches cast a spell to meet Macbeth.

❷ The witches prophesy Macbeth with be Thane of Cawdor and King
of Scotland.

❸ Banquo demands to learn his future – his offspring will be king.

❹ News arrives that Macbeth has been made Thane of Cawdor.

❺ Macbeth is preoccupied by thoughts of kingship.

The storm still attends the three witches as they gather to boast of
their exploits. They cast a spell as they prepare to meet Macbeth. He
arrives with Banquo and both are shocked by the appearance of the
witches. They greet Macbeth and inform him that he will become
Thane of Cawdor and also King of Scotland. Whilst Macbeth is
stunned by these prophecies, Banquo demands they inform him of his
future. He is told that although he will not be king, his offspring will
be. Macbeth recovers from his 'trance' and insists that the witches
explain how they know these things, since they are frankly incredible.
But the witches vanish as abruptly as they came.

The witches' boasting invokes evil but also reveals some limitations to
their powers. They may have the power to change shape, but the rat
has no tail (line 9) – in other words, is unnaturally and imperfectly
formed. Furthermore, in their attack upon the 'master o' the *Tiger*'
(line 7) they admit 'his bark cannot be lost' (line 24). What they do to
him, however, is reminiscent of Macbeth's future condition: 'dry as
hay' (line 18), sleepless (lines 19–22), and he will 'dwindle, peak, and

pine' (line 23). Note how keen Macbeth is to hear more of this 'strange intelligence' (line 75): 'Would they had stayed!' (line 81).

Macbeth and Banquo briefly discuss the 'insane' (line 83) revelations they have just heard, and at that point Ross and Angus arrive to convey thanks from King Duncan. Ross tells Macbeth he has become the Thane of Cawdor. Macbeth and Banquo are both amazed, and we begin to see Macbeth's ambition unfolding through the asides – or soliloquys – he delivers to the audience. Banquo warns of the danger of trusting such supernatural messages, but Macbeth is lost in his own thoughts, thinking through all the implications. Eventually, he is stirred and agrees to ride towards the king. In private to Banquo, he suggests they speak about the revelations at some future point, which Banquo agrees to.

> **CHECKPOINT 5**
>
> Why does Macbeth wish the witches had stayed?

Banquo's description of the witches is important in seeing how unnatural they are: they seem to be women but are not. It is Banquo who thinks they are evil: 'What! Can the devil speak true?' (line 106). Macbeth does not.

Banquo's warning to Macbeth concerning the 'instruments of darkness' (line 123) might also be construed as prophetic – Macbeth is betrayed as a result of believing these 'truths' (line 123), and he comes to realise this in his final confrontation with Macduff (V.6.58–61).

The **soliloquy** beginning 'Two truths are told' (line 126) shows that Macbeth all too quickly, following his accession as Thane of Cawdor, begins that process of imagining the steps he will need to take – that is, murdering Duncan – to become king. At this point the real horror of doing the deed seems to be balanced by a morbid fascination at its prospect.

The **imagery** of clothing – 'borrowed robes' (line 108) and 'strange garments' (line 145) – begins to be developed. This is significant because clothing is a powerful image suggesting concealment and disguise: Macbeth, as it were, hides behind his clothes of kingship.

> **The temptation of Macbeth**
>
> Here we meet Macbeth for the first time. And the brave, loyal soldier of Scene 2 is immediately fascinated – mesmerized even – by the 'instruments of darkness' (line 123).

SCENE 4 – King Duncan names his son, Malcolm, his heir

1. Duncan greets Macbeth and Banquo.
2. Duncan announces his intention to visit Macbeth's castle.
3. Duncan announces his son, Malcolm, as his successor.
4. Macbeth reveals his all-consuming ambition to be king.

King Duncan enquires of his son, Malcolm, about the execution of the Thane of Cawdor. He is told that Cawdor died repenting of his actions and with dignity. Macbeth and Banquo arrive and are profusely thanked by Duncan for their efforts. Duncan announces that his son, Malcolm, is to be his heir and also that he will visit Macbeth in his castle at Inverness. Macbeth leaves to prepare for the arrival of the king, but we learn that the announcement of Malcolm as heir is a bitter blow to him. In his absence, Duncan praises Macbeth to Banquo.

In this scene Macbeth's attitude to the murder has changed, even hardened. In Scene 3 the prospect, though desirable, was terrifying. His **soliloquy** (lines 49–54) reveals a new determination to carry it through. The vocabulary has switched from polysyllabic abstractions to largely monosyllabic matter-of-factness. **Couplets** clinch the sense of the line and the sense of inevitability about the deed Macbeth must do.

CHECKPOINT 6

How does the announcement of Malcolm as heir to the throne affect Macbeth?

 DID YOU KNOW?

Malcolm reigned as Malcolm III and his son, Duncan, became Duncan II.

Contrasts

The scene highlights a series of further contrasts: between Duncan and Banquo who are open and direct; and Macbeth who is covert in his intentions. Typically, for Duncan, stars shine (line 42), whereas for Macbeth they 'hide their fires' so that darkness prevails (lines 51–2). We also hear of the former Thane of Cawdor's noble death; this contrasts with the living Thane of Cawdor's ignoble ambition. Again, it is ironic that Duncan should comment concerning the former Thane of Cawdor that 'There's no art / To find the mind's construction in the face' (lines 12–13), since he so clearly fails to read what is in the new Thane of Cawdor's face. His trust of Macbeth leads to his death. The use of these contrasts serves to establish two contrary things: first, just how good and worthy a king Duncan is; second, just how appalling a crime it would be for Macbeth to murder him.

SCENE 5 – Lady Macbeth determined to be queen

1 Lady Macbeth hears of her husband's success, and the prophecies.

2 She determines she will assist him becoming king whatever the cost.

3 Macbeth appears and she begins the process of persuading him to murder Duncan.

Lady Macbeth reads a letter from her husband informing her of his success in battle and, more importantly, of his encounter with the witches. He believes their knowledge to be true, and communicates his excitement about his eventual destiny to be king – and so for her to be queen. After reading the letter, she is worried that Macbeth is too soft a person to be able to take the crown. She determines that she will assist him through 'the valour of my tongue' (line 25). On hearing – to her great surprise and then delight – that the king himself will be staying in their castle overnight, she exults and invokes demonic spirits to harden her own resolve and to destroy any

GLOSSARY

There's no art / To find the mind's construction in the face it's impossible to know what people are thinking from looking at their faces

weakness of pity. Macbeth enters and she immediately sets to work upon his intentions. He says little but she insists that the deed must be done, that she will personally organise its operation, and finally that failure to accomplish this act would be a form of fear.

DID YOU KNOW?

Lady Macbeth's real name was Gruoch (pronounced GROO-och). She was the granddaughter of a murdered Scottish king. Macbeth was her second husband.

Lady Macbeth

Lady Macbeth immediately understands the full implications of her husband's letter and her response is direct and uncompromising: her husband must be what he has been promised. No niceties of conscience or loyalty seem to assail her, and it is noticeable how she overwhelms her husband when he appears. It is also interesting to reflect how she instantly taps into the spirit world: her 'spirits' (line 24, an interesting plural) will invade Macbeth's ear, and she literally does invoke spirits to possess her body. The point about her 'unsex'-ing (line 39) and her 'woman's breasts' (line 45) no longer being used for milk but murder, bares a curious parallel with the ambiguous sexuality of the witches themselves. It is as if, at this level of evil, one abandons being either male or female – one is a neutral 'it'. Later (I.7.46), Macbeth himself, in trying to deflect his wife's arguments, puts forward the view that in daring/doing more than what is proper – or natural – for a man to do, one is no longer a man. Despite his argument, he, of course, does precisely that.

We have already seen the bloody nature of battle in Scene 2. The **imagery** of blood runs through the play. Look at what Lady Macbeth requests: 'Make thick my blood' (line 41). Here blood is seen as a natural function of the human body. One that naturally feeds man's capacity for compassion and repentance – things she wishes stopped.

The relationship between Macbeth and his wife

The letter to Lady Macbeth shows not only complete trust in his wife – for such a letter could itself be construed as treasonous – but also affection and love: 'my dearest partner of greatness' (lines 9–10) suggests a warm equality of persons. Later we will see how this affection cools.

SCENE 6 – Duncan arrives at Macbeth's castle

❶ Duncan arrives at Macbeth's castle and is greeted by Lady Macbeth.

King Duncan arrives at Macbeth's castle with his sons and attendant thanes. He admires the air. Lady Macbeth – without her husband – greets Duncan and they exchange pleasant courtesies. Duncan takes her hand and is led into the castle.

Once more the theme of reality versus appearances is lightly alluded to. The air and the castle appear delightful, but are in reality to be the site of foul murder.

Ironically, Duncan refers to Macbeth as the 'Thane of Cawdor' (line 20).

DID YOU KNOW?

In Shakespeare's time authority derived from God – in a 'great chain of being'. God was at the top. Then angels, mankind, animals, birds, fish and so on. In the human order the king was supreme. Males were above females.

CHECKPOINT 7

Appearances can be deceptive: where else is this very evident?

GLOSSARY

unsex me remove from me the weakness of being a woman. We see this traditional view of women's incapacity for murderous activities in Macduff's remark to her (II.3.80–3).

Make thick my blood prevent pity flowing through my veins

SCENE 7 – Macbeth debates whether to murder Duncan

❶ Macbeth debates whether he should kill Duncan.

❷ Lady Macbeth enters and mocks his indecisiveness and lack of masculinity.

❸ Macbeth commits to the murder.

DID YOU KNOW?

Historically, Banquo assisted Macbeth in killing Duncan!

As Macbeth's household prepares the feast for Duncan, Macbeth, alone, debates the pros and cons of murdering Duncan in his own mind. The biggest problem as he sees it is that murdering his own liege, kinsman and guest would set a precedent that would return to plague him. Also, he cannot dismiss the fact that Duncan has been such a good king – heaven itself will expose the wickedness of Macbeth. The only justification for the murder is, finally, his own ambition.

Macbeth – his guilt isolating him, and in some anguish as he seeks to decide what to do – reasons that if he could get away with the murder, then he wouldn't worry about damnation in the after-life. However, the imagery of his own imagination undermines his reasonings: as he considers Duncan's virtuous qualities, pictures of angels and cherubims seeking retribution assail and frighten him. Again, ironically, the initial hope that one blow would end the matter (lines 4–5) proves utterly false: the death of Duncan is swiftly followed by the illegal 'execution' of the two innocent guards.

His wife enters and he informs her he intends to change his mind and not murder Duncan – why should he throw away all the glory he has so recently gained? She is contemptuous of his change of heart and accuses him of cowardice. They argue but her violent resolution prevails – she outlines the plan – and he agrees to it.

EXAMINER'S SECRET

You will not get high marks simply by re-telling the story.

Lady Macbeth attacks her husband exactly where she knows it will hurt: his courage and manhood are at stake. And she does what she said she would do in Act I Scene 5, 'pour my spirits in thine ear' (I.5.24). Her strength of purpose and her leadership offer a remarkable contrast to Macbeth's performance at this stage. Notice how his final words in this scene, 'False face must hide what the false

heart doth know' (line 82), echo Lady Macbeth's earlier advice
(I.5.61–4).

Lady Macbeth's persuasiveness

This is the critical scene in which all the arguments against
treason and murder are explicitly and strongly made. Lady
Macbeth demolishes them all by questioning his manhood.

**CHECK
THE NET**

**www.
allshakespeare.
com/plays/macbeth**
is a good site for
commentary,
discussion and essays
on the play.

Now take a break!

WHO SAYS ...?

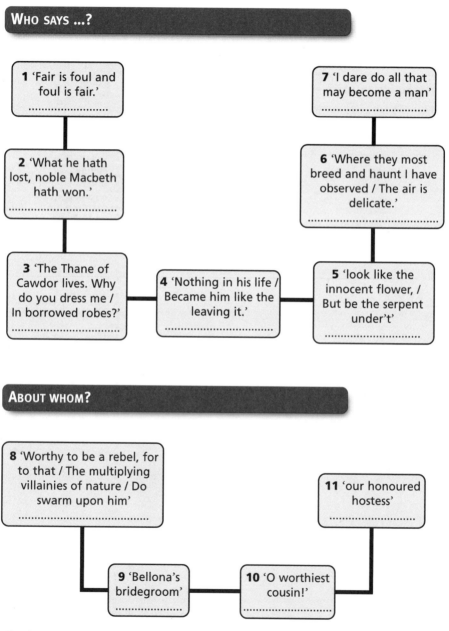

1 'Fair is foul and foul is fair.'
....

2 'What he hath lost, noble Macbeth hath won.'
....

3 'The Thane of Cawdor lives. Why do you dress me / In borrowed robes?'
....

4 'Nothing in his life / Became him like the leaving it.'
....

5 'look like the innocent flower, / But be the serpent under't'
....

6 'Where they most breed and haunt I have observed / The air is delicate.'
....

7 'I dare do all that may become a man'
....

ABOUT WHOM?

8 'Worthy to be a rebel, for to that / The multiplying villainies of nature / Do swarm upon him'
....

9 'Bellona's bridegroom'
....

10 'O worthiest cousin!'
....

11 'our honoured hostess'
....

Check your answers on p. 92.

SCENE 1 – Macbeth and Banquo meet briefly

1 Banquo has a premonition that something is wrong.

2 He meets Macbeth and they discuss the witches.

3 After Banquo retires, Macbeth, alone, imagines he sees a dagger leading him towards Duncan's chamber.

4 As the bell rings, Macbeth resolves to kill Duncan.

Banquo is out walking late with his son, Fleance. He cannot sleep and feels some premonition that something is wrong. The introduction of Banquo at this point allows us another point of contrast with Macbeth. We see the witches have affected him too – but whereas Macbeth has surrendered his will to them, Banquo's dreams are invaded. Banquo senses something is wrong, but he does not know what.

EXAMINER'S SECRET
A typical examination answer might use as many as eight quotations.

Banquo encounters Macbeth and presents him with a diamond for Macbeth's wife, a gift from the king. The gift of the diamond, especially to Lady Macbeth, underlines further the monstrous ingratitude of Macbeth himself, and rams home another **irony**: that Duncan has failed again to read 'the mind's construction in the face' (I.4.12–14), for it is Lady Macbeth who has ensured he is to be killed.

Banquo tells Macbeth that he dreamt of the witches. Macbeth dismisses thoughts of them, but requests that he and Banquo speak about the matter another time. Banquo agrees but not without the reservation that honour should not be comprised.

Macbeth's request to talk of the witches later with its promise to 'make honour for you' (line 26) is an attempt to sound Banquo out – how will he react should the status quo change? Banquo's answer, which insists upon maintaining integrity, is hardly likely to please Macbeth. Banquo cannot be bought. It is not surprising that later Macbeth comments that he feels 'rebuked' (III.1.55) by him.

CHECKPOINT 8

How does Banquo appear more open than Macbeth?

Macbeth is left alone and imagines he sees a dagger in front of him – a dagger which guides him towards the goal he seeks of killing Duncan. Initially he experiences horror at the reality of what he is contemplating, but this gives way to resolution. As the bell rings, he determines to proceed forward and kill Duncan.

NOTE: THE SCENE OF THE MURDER IS NOT SHOWN ON STAGE.

SCENE 2 – Macbeth murders King Duncan

1 Having drugged the guards, Lady Macbeth waits for her husband's return from the murder.

2 Macbeth returns having killed Duncan, but is extremely troubled.

3 Lady Macbeth upbraids him for having brought the murder weapons back with him.

4 She plants the weapons on the guards.

5 They retire to bed on hearing knocking on the castle gate.

We do not see the actual murder on stage. Instead, prior to the murder we are made most aware of the vision of the dagger leading Macbeth on; and after the murder we are most conscious of sounds which disturb the peace. The murder is, as it were, sandwiched between intense sensory experiences – we are meant to 'feel' it happening.

Nerves on edge, Lady Macbeth waits for Macbeth to return from having done the murder. Her mood is exultant and bold, and she boasts how she has drugged the guards. She would have murdered Duncan herself, except his sleeping form reminded her of her father.

Macbeth enters, carrying two bloodstained daggers.

He is obsessed by the noises he has heard, and particularly is distressed by the fact that when passing Malcolm and Donalbain's chamber he was unable to say 'amen' in response to their request for blessing. The guilt of what he has done torments him, and Lady Macbeth attempts to allay and rationalise his fears.

The fact that such a great warrior – and killer of men – is so lost in terrifying guilt indicates the full extent of the evil he has committed. Earlier in the play, Macbeth wanted to 'jump the life to come' (I.7.7) – as if there were no divine retribution he need worry about. Now, the need for 'Amen' (line 28), which he cannot speak and the fact that even the ocean cannot clean him, suggests a state of total damnation.

EXAMINER'S SECRET

A planned answer is always rewarded.

CHECKPOINT 9

What state of mind is Macbeth in?

CHECK THE FILM

The actual murder of Duncan is not physically shown on stage in the text of the play. However, the 1971 Roman Polanski film version of *Macbeth* shows it in harrowing detail.

Lady Macbeth focuses on the need to keep to the plan of action – ordering him to go back and place the daggers beside the guards, so as to incriminate them. Macbeth, however, is too terrified to return. Lady Macbeth undertakes the deed and leaves him there alone. A knocking at the castle gate further disturbs his state of mind. Lady Macbeth reenters. As the knocking continues she advises that he pulls himself together and that they retire to bed, so as not to be seen up and about when the murder is discovered.

Irony is ever present. Lady Macbeth imagines that washing one's hands will wash away guilt: it is she, finally (V.1.42), who is unable to wash her hands clean. And her comment to Macbeth, 'Infirm of purpose!' (line 52), comes back to haunt her, as he strengthens in evil resolve, whilst she becomes madly suicidal – anticipated in her dismissive comment 'so, it will make us mad' (line 34).

> ### Lady Macbeth's resolve
>
> Despite some nervous apprehension early on – Lady Macbeth is entirely in control of herself and of her husband. She planned the execution, and now it is her readiness of mind and strength of purpose that compensate for Macbeth's failure to act decisively once the murder is committed.

DID YOU KNOW?

Macbeth is one of Shakespeare's shortest plays (only *The Comedy of Errors* and *The Tempest* are shorter) and one reason is because there is no subplot.

SCENE 3 – The murder of Duncan is discovered

❶ The Porter lets in Macduff and Lennox.

❷ Macbeth, feigning to be woken, greets them and takes them to Duncan's chamber.

❸ The murder is discovered and Macbeth in a false display of loyalty blames and kills the guards without trial.

❹ Malcolm and Donalbain suspect Macbeth and prepare to flee.

The knocking from the previous scene continues and the Porter, hungover from the night's feast, goes to open the gate. As he does so, he imagines he is the porter of hell. He lets in Macduff and Lennox.

The role of the Porter

The bleak intensity of the previous scene gives way to a brief comic interlude. Although the Porter is crude and rough, and his introduction is intended to make us laugh, yet his role also performs other important functions. The continuation of physical knocking reminds us that we are still in the world where the Macbeths commit murder. Therefore, the Porter's self-appointed role as a hell-porter is not so fanciful. Earlier we have seen references to serpents (I.5.64) and chalices (I.7.11) and with that the suggestion that the Devil has entered into Macbeth. Later, Macduff is to say that Macbeth is a devil (IV.3.56). Literally, then, it would seem, there is hell where Macbeth is. And, more interestingly still, much of the Porter's speeches are connected to contemporary events: namely, the Gunpowder Plot and its own enormity of treason. Thus, whilst making some good-humoured jokes, the overall thrust of the Porter's remarks is to widen the application of the play – hell is not only on the stage in Macbeth's castle, but present in the society for which Shakespeare was writing. Furthermore, we already know that the murder has been committed – this delay in its discovery heightens the tension and our sense of anticipation.

Seemingly awoken by their knocking, Macbeth comes forward to greet them. Macduff asks to be led to the king. While he enters the king's chamber, Lennox comments to Macbeth on how stormy the night was. Lennox's account of the storm is counterpointed by an almost dismissive four-word reply (line 57) from Macbeth: ''Twas a rough night'. In that tiny detail we see how unable Macbeth is to be natural and sociable. He has no time for ordinary conversation – he is keyed up and waiting for the outburst he knows must come from Macduff.

Macduff, discovering the murder, returns, loudly proclaiming treason. As Macduff proceeds to stir the castle, Macbeth and Lennox rush in to ascertain the facts for themselves. Lady Macbeth appears, then Banquo, and both are informed of the reason for the commotion. Typically, in a world of inverted values, Lady Macbeth's first concern on 'learning' that Duncan has been murdered is that it reflects badly

EXAMINER'S SECRET

Always read the whole examination paper before you start writing.

GLOSSARY

Infirm of purpose wavering, weak in intention

Scene 3 continued

on 'our house' (line 85). Equally typically, it is Banquo who provides a more sensitive perspective.

Macbeth returns and emotionally bemoans the dreadful deed. At this point Malcolm and Donalbain arrive and are informed rhetorically by Macbeth, and then directly by Macduff, that their father has been murdered. Lennox suggests the guards may have been responsible, and it emerges Macbeth immediately slew them. Macduff questions this, and as Macbeth justifies his actions, his wife faints and attention is distracted to her. It can be argued that Macbeth's justification for killing the two guards becomes so colourful and rhetorical that he is in danger of being exposed through what might be considered 'overacting' his part. Lady Macbeth's swoon, therefore, at this point conveniently distracts attention away from her husband and the question he poses (lines 113–5). Perhaps, from his point of view, it is best left unanswered.

CHECKPOINT 10

Why does Macbeth slay the guards?

Banquo assumes command and directs them to meet in readiness. As they exit from stage, Malcolm and Donalbain remain: they decide to flee – suspecting treachery from someone closely related.

Donalbain and Malcolm's decision to flee clearly plays into Macbeth's hand. However, that does not mean it is a bad decision. To have stayed may well have led to their own assassinations. As they observe, the 'nea'er in blood / The nearer bloody' (lines 137–8). This can only mean they suspect Macbeth.

> **Hell discovered**
>
> This pivotal scene anticipates the horror of Macbeth's reign: the 'hell' the Porter mentions (line 2) becomes a reality. Deception, murder, distrust, fear and flight abound.

SCENE 4 – Macbeth named king

1 An Old Man discusses with Ross the unnatural omens of the time.

2 Macduff enters and informs them Duncan's sons are suspected of the crime and Macbeth is to be crowned king.

3 Macduff says he will not attend the investiture.

Ross and an Old Man recall the dreadful night of the murder. The Old Man states that he cannot remember a parallel to it. As they discuss the unnatural state of things, darkness indeed seems to have usurped the place of light. The scene gives us a breathing space before we meet the new king, Macbeth; and further, it acts as a commentary on all that has happened. The importance of the Old Man lies simply in his being a representative of the people, and one whose memory goes back a long way – the crimes committed are without parallel. Ross describes the extent of the darkness and this again **symbolically** reminds us of Christ's crucifixion and the great darkness that enveloped the land.

Macduff enters and brings them up to date with the news. Duncan's two sons are suspected of paying the guards to commit the murder precisely because they have now fled. Macbeth has been nominated king and has gone to Scone to be invested. Ross asks Macduff whether he will go to the investiture. Macduff says he will not, but will return home to Fife. Ross himself intends to go. They all part and the Old Man pronounces a blessing.

Macduff's suspicions concerning Macbeth are revealed by two facts: the dry observation that the murderers were 'Those that Macbeth hath slain' (line 22) – and so could not be questioned – and that he will not go to Scone for the coronation. This contrasts with Ross's readiness to go and to align himself with the new regime.

CHECKPOINT 11

How important to the play is the character of Duncan?

 DID YOU KNOW?

Macbeth has traditionally been considered an 'unlucky' play. It is referred to as 'The Scottish Play' by the players.

Now take a break!

Who says ...?

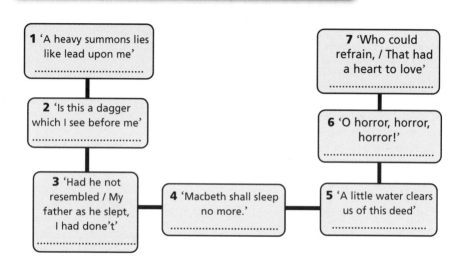

1 'A heavy summons lies like lead upon me'
....

2 'Is this a dagger which I see before me'
....

3 'Had he not resembled / My father as he slept, I had done't'
....

4 'Macbeth shall sleep no more.'
....

5 'A little water clears us of this deed'
....

6 'O horror, horror, horror!'
....

7 'Who could refrain, / That had a heart to love'
....

About whom?

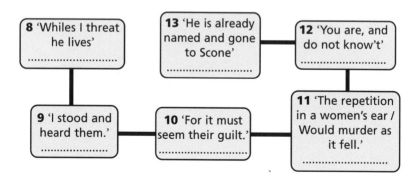

8 'Whiles I threat he lives'
....

9 'I stood and heard them.'
....

10 'For it must seem their guilt.'
....

11 'The repetition in a women's ear / Would murder as it fell.'
....

12 'You are, and do not know't'
....

13 'He is already named and gone to Scone'
....

Check your answers on p. 92.

SCENE 1 – Banquo reflects on witches' words

① Banquo, alone, suspects Macbeth's involvement in the murder of Duncan.

② Macbeth and Lady Macbeth arrive and remind Banquo he is chief guest at their feast.

③ Macbeth ascertains details of Banquo's (and Fleance's) horseriding journey.

④ Macbeth fears Banquo and entertains two murderers to assassinate both Banquo and Fleance, his son.

Banquo, alone, reflects on the witches' prophecies, and suspects that Macbeth did indeed obtain the crown through treachery. But given that the prophecies have all come true for Macbeth, he reasons there is hope for his family. Although Banquo is immune to the temptation that the witches' prophecies afford, he is not immune to the prophecies themselves. They clearly disturb his peace of mind, and although there is no suggestion that he will 'help' the prophecies come true (as Macbeth did), he nevertheless begins to incline towards their 'truth'. This contrasts – in the same scene – with Macbeth's obsession that they will come true, and therefore that he (Macbeth) must stop them. Macbeth's comments on Banquo later in this scene give us much information about the character of Banquo: what emerges is his courage, wisdom and integrity.

DID YOU KNOW?

On the one hand, Macbeth believes the prophecies must come true, and on the other, he seeks to prevent them happening!

Macbeth and Lady Macbeth and their entourage arrive. They remind Banquo he is their chief guest at their banquet that evening. Macbeth feigns that he needs Banquo's advice on the following day on how to deal with Malcolm and Donalbain, who are abroad and spreading rumours. He elicits from Banquo details of his journey and that Fleance will be with him. Macbeth then dismisses everyone. Alone, Macbeth reveals that he fears Banquo, and that the thought that Banquo's offspring should become kings is entirely unacceptable to him. This is the first time we see Macbeth as king. Immediately we discover the kind of king he is going to be: entirely duplicitous – the appearance of an innocent flower, but really the serpent under it (I.5.63–4). Under the guise of appearing to honour and value his erstwhile comrade-in-arms, he casually ascertains his movements that

night and confirms that Fleance will be with him. All this is to entrap
and murder him and his child.

**EXAMINER'S
SECRET**
To gain the best
grade there is no
need to write reams!

Two murderers whom he wishes to see are brought in. To them he
vehemently outlines why Banquo is their mutual enemy, and they
agree to perform the murder. The depths to which Macbeth has sunk
are clear in his conversation with the murderers: here is a great
warrior-hero – 'Bellona's bridegroom' (I.2.56) – who now has to meet
the most vicious and corrupt kind of men in secret in order to both
disguise and obtain his ends. The fact that he himself despises these
men is shown in the way he addresses them – the interruption of the
first murderer's solemn declaration of loyalty with the ironic 'Your
spirits shine through you' (line 127) points to contempt.
Subsequently, the mission of the third murderer (Act III Scene 3)
shows how little he actually trusts the first two. But, then, trust is no
longer something Macbeth believes in. Crucially, in the next scene
(Act III Scene 2), even Lady Macbeth is not privy to his plans.

It is worth noting the bestial **imagery** with which men can be
classified in the same way as dogs. We remember that before he 'fell',
Macbeth said he dared do all that a man should do – to do more was
to be no man (I.7.46–7). In other words, acting like an animal is a
natural consequence of his choices – and the imagery demonstrates
that.

SCENE 2 – Macbeth will commit another crime

❶ Lady Macbeth is uneasy; her husband spends his time alone.

❷ They discuss the threat Banquo and Fleance pose to their reign.

❸ Macbeth discloses another dreadful crime he intends to commit,
and asks her to applaud his actions when it's done.

Lady Macbeth wants to speak to her husband before the feast. She is
not happy – uncertainty and insecurity trouble them both. Macbeth
appears and she upbraids him for both staying alone and for his
continual dwelling on the actions they have done. Macbeth envies the
peaceful dead. Lady Macbeth attempts to cheer him up. They discuss

the feast ahead, resolve to praise Banquo at it, and then Macbeth reveals his fear of Banquo and Fleance. He then further reveals that he intends to commit another dreadful crime. He will not tell her what it is, but asks her to praise it when it's achieved. Lady Macbeth is amazed but drawn along with him.

Lady Macbeth begins to lose charge

For Macbeth this proves an incubation period in which he grows stronger – 'Things bad begun make strong themselves by ill' (line 55) – and inures himself to doing evil; for Lady Macbeth it is the start of her disintegration – she will take control one more time, at the banquet (Act III Scene 4), and then she will be overwhelmed by remorse for the tide of evil she has helped unleash, and go mad. Their roles are reversing.

In the encounters so far, Lady Macbeth has been dominant. Now we see the situation changing. Macbeth is keeping himself to himself and brooding on the crimes committed, and on the crimes he intends to commit – notice the bestial **imagery** again: 'O, full of scorpions is my mind' (line 35). Furthermore, he is not sharing his thoughts with his wife (I.5.9–10) and so she is feeling isolated. This despite the affectionate term – 'dearest chuck' (line 45) – Macbeth uses for her.

EXAMINER'S SECRET

If you are asked to make a comparison, use comparing words or phrases: e.g. however, whereas, by contrast, on the other hand.

SCENE 3 – Murderers kill Banquo

1 The two murderers are joined by a third.

2 They murder Banquo, but Fleance escapes.

3 They go to report what they have done to Macbeth.

The two murderers are joined by a third. They await Banquo and Fleance's approach, spring out and manage to assassinate Banquo. In the confusion Fleance escapes. The murderers resolve to inform Macbeth of what has been done.

GLOSSARY

Things bad begun make strong themselves by ill evil strengthens itself by committing more evil

DID YOU KNOW?

The identity of the third murderer has caused much debate. Some have even suggested it is Macbeth in disguise! After all, how would he know 'but he [Banquo] does usually'? The 'So all men do' (III.3.12–13) may be a cover-up.

The addition of a third murderer adds nothing to the progress of the plot, but exposes the kind of world Macbeth inhabits and creates all around him: 'He needs not our mistrust' (line 2). Macbeth trusts no one, not even the accomplices he has commissioned. In the next scene (Act III Scene 4) we learn he has spies everywhere – everyone is being checked.

Notice the night and day contrasts which run through the play. The loss of light foreshadows the loss of life.

SCENE 4 – Murdered Banquo's ghost appears at feast

❶ At the banquet Macbeth welcomes his guests.

❷ Macbeth steps aside to speak to the first murderer in order to learn Banquo is indeed dead.

❸ Banquo's ghost appears and terrifies Macbeth – only Lady Macbeth's quick thinking saves the situation.

❹ The ghost appears a second time and Lady Macbeth has to dismiss the assembly.

❺ Recomposing himself, Macbeth reveals Macduff's opposition and his intention to visit the witches again.

Macbeth welcomes various guests to his banquet. The first murderer appears and Macbeth steps aside to speak with him. He learns that Banquo is dead, but that Fleance escaped – this disturbs him. He returns to the feast and is gently upbraided by his wife for his absence.

As he stands, making a speech praising Banquo, Banquo's ghost takes the only remaining chair. Banquo's ghost, **ironically** occupies Macbeth's seat – as his descendants will his throne – 'push us from our stools' (line 81). Only Macbeth can see the ghost and he is terrified – only Lady Macbeth's quick thinking covers up the fact that Macbeth is beginning to reveal his guilt. The ghost disappears and Macbeth regains his composure. Once more he attempts good cheer and invokes the name of Banquo: the ghost reappears and Macbeth loses his nerve altogether. He recovers himself when the ghost disappears again, but too late to enable the banquet to continue. Lady Macbeth heads off a question from Ross and dismisses everyone.

The dramatic tension in this scene is brilliantly exploited. First, the appearance of the murderer (albeit on the fringes) is itself shocking – perhaps one needs to consider this in modern terms: it would be like a street gangster appearing in the doorway of a State banquet. The risks to Macbeth in being seen with such a person are enormous – and this gives a clear indication of his state of mind. Macbeth *has* to

CHECK THE NET

www. allshakespeare. com is good for a whole range of useful material on Shakespeare educational videos, interactive CDs, and one-page plays (these contain the whole play text on one 32x45 inch sheet!).

know that Banquo and Fleance are dead, whatever the consequences. As he says later in the scene: 'For mine own good / All causes shall give way' (lines 134–5). Second, the tension is exploited by the way that Macbeth in fact reveals – almost plainly – his guilt, but on each occasion Lady Macbeth is able ingeniously to bale him out. We are kept on tenterhooks: will he be exposed? And she just manages to keep him ahead of it.

Alone with his wife, Macbeth confides that Macduff seems to be standing against him. He reveals, too, that he has spies everywhere, and that he intends to revisit the witches.

> ### Witchcraft and psychology
>
> This scene raises the interesting question of witchcraft and psychology. Certainly, the supernatural **motif** is superbly developed: we have had the witches, their prophecies, the dagger that led Macbeth to Duncan, and now we have the ghost of Banquo. But whereas Banquo saw and heard the witches alongside Macbeth, here only Macbeth sees the vision. As Lady Macbeth says, 'When all's done / You look but on a stool' (line 66–7). This has practical implications for any production of the play – is the ghost in the mind of Macbeth solely (and so is not shown on stage), or does a ghost really appear? Perhaps because of its sheer dramatic impact, most versions of the play tend to want to include it.

The strain on Lady Macbeth is evident. Although he has been terrified, Macbeth, by the end of the scene, seems casual in his attitude to what has happened. His comment, 'We are yet but young in deed' (line 143) suggests that this mere blip will soon pass. She, however, has had to use all her resources and wit to contain the potential damage of exposure. Earlier she had said 'Naught's had, all's spent' (III.2.5) and we see this particularly in this scene: she wanted to be queen and the scene begins with her keeping 'her state' (line 5), in other words, remaining on her throne. If there was anywhere in the play where the full enjoyment of majesty could be entertained, it is here: Lady Macbeth on her throne, surrounded by subjects. Yet this, through Macbeth's actions, becomes a hollow and empty event,

CHECKPOINT 12

What do you think the thanes would be thinking after the banquet?

DID YOU KNOW?

The word 'weird' originally meant 'destiny' or 'fate'. The three weird sisters remind us of the three Fates of Greek mythology (Clotho, Lachesis and Atropo).

lacking any dignity or regal significance. Perhaps it is no wonder, lacking any other significance in her life, that her mind then does begin to question the value of what it has accomplished. Macbeth, we notice, no longer talks of the *we* – himself and his partner of greatness – but of himself alone: 'For mine own good / All causes shall give way' (lines 134–5).

The reference once more to sleep (line 140) reinforces our sense of their guilt, but also points to the **dramatic irony** that Macbeth himself is a prophet: 'Macbeth shall sleep no more' (II.2.43).

Macbeth's high point

At this moment Macbeth has achieved his ambition and maximum control. At the start of the scene the thanes, excepting Macduff, are disposed to accept him as their legitimate king – but the appearance of the ghost at this point of triumph marks his decline. All is downhill for him from now on.

SCENE 5 – WITCHES PREPARE TO MEET MACBETH AGAIN

● **The three witches and the goddess of witchcraft, Hecate, prepare a strong spell for deluding Macbeth.**

The suggestion that Macbeth is a 'son' (line 11), albeit 'wayward', suggests that Macbeth is no longer a victim of the witches' evil, but more an adept – one of them – in their art. However, there can be no doubt – adept or not – by the end of the play he has so fully embraced evil, he has destroyed himself.

The need for 'strength' (line 28) is reflected in the witches' offering to let Macbeth see their 'masters' (IV.1.62).

 DID YOU KNOW?

In 1604 the English Parliament passed a law against witchcraft. It said, 'If any person shall use any invocation or conjuration of any evil or wicked spirit; or shall consult, covenant with, entertain, employ, feed or reward any evil or cursed spirit to or for any intent … that every such person being convicted shall suffer death.'

GLOSSARY

We are yet but young in deed we are only novices in evil at the moment

Naught's had, all's spent we have achieved nothing and lost everything

Scene 6 – The political situation in Scotland

1 Two nobles of Scotland discuss the deaths of Duncan and Banquo.

2 Lennox supports the army Malcolm is raising in England.

EXAMINER'S SECRET

Always check your answers when you have finished.

CHECKPOINT 13

What sense of resistance is there to Macbeth's rule?

Lennox outlines to another lord in deeply **ironic** terms his understanding of what has been happening in Scotland: i.e. that Macbeth is responsible for all the murders that have plagued the state. Malcolm is in the English court attempting to raise military support to reclaim his throne. Macduff is in disgrace for refusing to attend Macbeth's banquet and is attempting to join Malcolm.

Macbeth earlier had said he intended to 'send' for Macduff (III.4.129) and this scene briefly covers the fact that he has – Macduff has simply refused point-blank to attend.

Now take a break!

WHO SAYS ...?

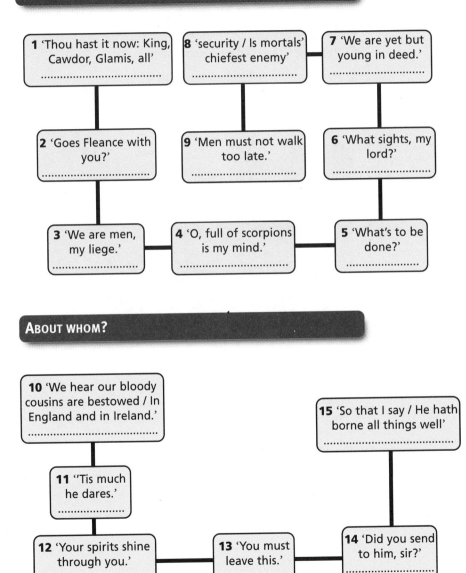

1 'Thou hast it now: King, Cawdor, Glamis, all'
....

8 'security / Is mortals' chiefest enemy'
....

7 'We are yet but young in deed.'
....

2 'Goes Fleance with you?'
....

9 'Men must not walk too late.'
....

6 'What sights, my lord?'
....

3 'We are men, my liege.'
....

4 'O, full of scorpions is my mind.'
....

5 'What's to be done?'
....

ABOUT WHOM?

10 'We hear our bloody cousins are bestowed / In England and in Ireland.'
....

15 'So that I say / He hath borne all things well'
....

11 ''Tis much he dares.'
....

12 'Your spirits shine through you.'
....

13 'You must leave this.'
....

14 'Did you send to him, sir?'
....

Check your answers on p. 92.

SCENE 1 – Witches prophesy three things to Macbeth

1. **Macbeth receives three prophecies from the witches.**
2. **He learns Banquo's descendants will be kings.**
3. **He determines to kill Macduff and his family.**

 CHECK THE FILM

Orson Welles's version of *Macbeth* (1948) became known as the 'voodoo' *Macbeth*. Set in the Caribbean, the film creates a dark and menacing atmosphere.

Three witches cast a spell and prepare to meet Macbeth. Hecate and three other witches appear and Hecate approves the work of the first three witches, and then disappears with the three she has brought with her. The supernatural atmosphere is charged with evil. The witches' spells are particularly nauseating in the level of detail they depict – here, if any further proof were needed, is evidence of precisely how unnatural these hags are.

Prior to his arrival, Macbeth is described as 'Something wicked' (line 45) – not even someone. Macbeth is one of their ilk now. This is in line with the overall effect of evil in dehumanising the personality – the bestial **imagery** commented upon is also a manifestation of this. So is the fact that they do a 'deed without a name' (line 48).

Macbeth then enters and commands them to answer his questions. They call up powerful spirits to respond to him. He is told three prophecies: that he should fear Macduff, that he cannot be harmed by one born of a woman and that he is secure until Birnan Wood comes to Dunsinane. He then presses them for more information about Banquo's offspring and is mortified to see a vision of eight kings all descended from Banquo, who also appears. The witches suddenly vanish and Macbeth curses them. Lennox appears and informs Macbeth that Macduff has fled to England. Macbeth determines to kill Macduff's wife and children as a reprisal.

Earlier uncertainties have been stripped away. Before, the witches informed him of the prophecies; now he demands of them what he wants to know. He even threatens the powerful master spirits with a curse if they do not answer him (line 104). And when he leaves, there is no more agonising about what he needs to do – or discussing the situation with his wife – Macduff's castle is to be attacked. An incidental point here is the depths to which Macbeth has fallen in murdering, without any compunction, women and children.

One consequence of his visit is the certainty of 'security' (III.5.32), which has troubled Macbeth from the outset. One factor in establishing the trustworthiness of the prophecies in Macbeth's mind is the speed with which they happen: 'Cawdor' (I.3.104) followed immediately upon their pronunciation of it; now, having been told to watch out for Macduff, Lennox appears with the same warning. Of course, the irony is that all the prophecies are double-edged and turn against him. Banquo's comment accurately reflects the truth: 'The instruments of darkness tell us truths; / Win us with honest trifles, to betray's / In deepest consequence' (I.3.123–5). These words are prophetic and an indictment of all that Macbeth comes to believe.

 DID YOU KNOW?

The ingredients of the witches' spell are especially revolting. For example, 'grease, that's sweaten / From the murderer's gibbet' (IV.1.65–6) refers to liquified body fat which breaks through the cracked skin of a body that's been hanging on the gallows for over a week. Often there was a puddle directly underneath the hanging corpse.

SCENE 2 – Lady Macduff and her son murdered

① **Ross warns but abandons Lady Macduff and her son.**

② **Lady Macduff and her son are murdered.**

Lady Macduff is with her son and Ross. Ross informs her that her husband has fled to England. Lady Macduff accuses her husband of cowardice. Ross makes his excuses and leaves. Ross is sympathetic, but cleverly manages not to be present when the murderers arrive. Ross always seems to be on the 'right' side of things.

The son interrogates his mother about the meaning of the word traitor. The discussion on traitors is highly pertinent – the real traitor, of course, is Macbeth. The discussion with her son, though, points us towards a consideration of all forms of loyalty, domestic as well as political. Although Lady Macduff berates her husband's cowardice, in front of the murderers she shows courage and defends her husband.

CHECKPOINT 14

Is Macduff a coward?

A messenger abruptly arrives, warns of danger, and leaves. Murderers enter, kill her son, and pursue her with the same purpose. A small point, but these murderers, compared with those who murdered Banquo, are far more savage and brutal. This too indicates the increasing degradation of Macbeth.

The scene is particularly affecting because Lady Macduff and her son are entirely innocent of any crime. At least with the murder of Banquo and the attempted murder of Fleance, Macbeth had a 'reason' for it. Here there is no such justification.

It is not coincidental that the desire to eliminate all unfortunates that 'trace him in his line' (IV.1.152) immediately follows Macbeth's vision of the line of Banquo as kings – clearly, the thought of dynasty obsesses and torments Macbeth. The scene is also affecting because the dialogue between Lady Macduff and her son reveals two delightful human beings: the waste of life that Macbeth's ambition has incurred is more fully realised in this snapshot of two good people about to be 'snuffed' out, than in all the talk about the stifling and tyrannical political atmosphere of Scotland under his reign.

We do not see Lady Macduff murdered on stage (unlike her son), but we do see and further hear her screaming '*Murder*' as she flees offstage. This seems a particularly brilliant piece of staging that reinforces a central **thematic** idea. To have had her murdered onstage would have created a moment of fear and suspense, but the execution would have been over immediately, and another dead body left on the stage. To have her fleeing offstage, screaming murder, is to prolong that sense of imminent fear and to leave it ringing in our ears – in fact, it is to leave us in uncertainty till we learn the truth in the next scene. This is a natural consequence of the kind of fear that Macbeth himself detests – not knowing, not being sure. His reign has created this unease for everybody. The insecurity and uncertainty becomes a tangible phenomenon (through the sound) for the audience watching the play.

CHECK THE NET

Look at **www. shakespeare. about.com** for a guide on the top ten Shakespeare books to buy.

> ### Even-handed justice
>
> Just as Lady Macduff goes off stage screaming to her death, so Lady Macbeth screams off stage as she takes her own life. In Lady Macbeth's case, of course, Macbeth hears it. The train of events he has started effectively return to his own family.

EXAMINER'S SECRET

The exam booklets contain enough paper for you to get the highest marks!

SCENE 3 – Malcolm and Macduff discuss kingship

1 **In England Malcolm tests Macduff's loyalty.**

2 **News arrives that Macduff's family has been wiped out.**

3 **Macduff swears revenge against Macbeth.**

This scene provides a balance to the others in Act IV. The evil of Macbeth's visit to the witches, and the dreadful murder of the Macduffs, now gives way to more 'normal' emotions and reactions.

CHECKPOINT 15

Why does Malcolm pretend he is more depraved than Macbeth?

In England, Malcolm entertains Macduff: Malcolm pretends that he is even more depraved than Macbeth, and so should not ascend the throne. Malcolm is suspicious of Macduff – neither of them at the beginning of the scene know what Macbeth has done to Macduff's family. One cause of Malcolm's suspicion is, as he says, 'He hath not touched you yet' (line 14), meaning that Macbeth has not injured Macduff's family (a **dramatic irony** in the circumstances of the preceding scene), and so why should Macduff quarrel with Macbeth? Malcolm has already experienced traitors who have tried to entrap him (lines 117–20), and so is wary of committing himself.

EXAMINER'S SECRET

Always write a plan for every answer. It ensures you answer the question and stops you from waffling.

Macduff's lament for Scotland, however, convinces Malcolm – who then retracts his confessions of evil – that Macduff is sincere and opposed to Macbeth. He reveals to Macduff that he has English support for an invasion of Scotland. Macduff is confused but pleased by this turn of events. A doctor appears and mentions the saintly work of King Edward the Confessor. After he leaves, Malcolm and Macduff discuss the true virtues of kingship, and how this is transmitted to succeeding monarchs. The reference to the way a monarch might cure the King's Evil (Scrofula) with a touch and how this gift is passed on is surely present not only to contrast with Macbeth's cursed reign, but also to gratify King James, who saw himself as having this gift.

Ross arrives with news and eventually, reluctantly, informs Macduff that his family has been murdered. Macduff is temporarily overwhelmed by the news, but collects himself. He is resolved to support Malcolm and vows to kill Macbeth himself.

The scene, although full of dramatic tension – as Malcolm plays his game with Macduff, and as Ross enters, reluctant to reveal the truth – is largely static: it concludes with the action they are going to take. So it is important as a springboard into Act V. But equally, it is important in the number of dramatic contrasts it provides. Of fundamental importance is the contrast between King Macbeth and King Edward. Also, we should bear in mind here that Malcolm will be king – and we see the kind of man he is, the values he possesses, and there is another reference to remind us how good Duncan was.

Further, there are other personal contrasts that should be noted: Macduff's reaction to the death of his wife might usefully be compared with Macbeth's reaction (V.5.17–27). Such a contrast will show how desensitised Macbeth has become to all normal human feeling. Finally, in trying to understand human character, we might want to ask why Ross, in relating the death of Macduff's family, omits to mention his own presence and conversation with Lady Macduff and his 'cousin' (IV.2.25) shortly before.

DID YOU KNOW?

This scene is important as it explores the issues of kingship.

> **The Opposition**
>
> This scene is important because it establishes the integrity of Malcolm and Macduff. The world of Macbeth and the witches is wholly dark – this scene provides a welcome contrast.

Now take a break!

WHO SAYS ...?

1 'Say if thou'dst rather hear it from our mouths / Or from our masters'
....

2 'No boasting like a fool'
....

3 'He loves us not.'
....

4 'I am not treacherous.'
....

5 'But I have none. / The king-becoming graces'
....

6 'They were all struck for thee.'
....

7 'Macbeth is ripe for shaking'
....

ABOUT WHOM?

8 'O well done! I commend your pains'
....

9 'His flight was madness'
....

10 'Why in that rawness left you wife and child'
....

11 'If such a one be fit to govern, speak.'
....

12 'Such sanctity hath heaven given this hand'
....

Check your answers on p. 92.

SCENE 1 – Lady Macbeth reveals her guilt while asleep

1 **Lady Macbeth is observed sleepwalking by her doctor and nurse.**

2 **The guilt of Lady Macbeth is evident – as is her mental torture.**

In Macbeth's castle at Dunsinane a doctor and a waiting-gentlewoman discuss their patient, Lady Macbeth. The gentlewoman refuses to discuss what she has heard Lady Macbeth say in her sleep, since she has no witness to corroborate her statements. As the doctor attempts to persuade her, Lady Macbeth appears, sleepwalking. They both hear her reveal her guilt and watch her futile attempts to remove the blood from her hands. The doctor concludes that she is more in need of spiritual rather than medical attention.

The clear mental breakdown of Lady Macbeth is both deeply affecting and also strikes the audience, in psychological terms, as profoundly true. There are a number of points to notice. First, as with all guilt, there is the obsession with the past. Remember, it was Lady Macbeth who said, 'what's done is done' (III.2.12), thus suggesting that it would no longer be of concern. Here, despite all her courage and ambition and strength of purpose, all that has been 'done' is not past, but present – and ever present – in her mind. She

> **CHECKPOINT 16**
>
> Why can't the nurse report what she has heard Lady Macbeth say?

herself refers to her own earlier declaration when she says, 'What's done cannot be undone' (lines 62–3).

The contrast with Macbeth himself could not be more marked – 'I cannot taint with fear' (V.3.3). Until the prophecies start unravelling, Macbeth seems impervious to concern.

DID YOU KNOW?

After the Restoration of Charles II, the language of Shakespeare went out of fashion. Shakespeare's godson, William Davenant, produced versions of the plays which supplanted Shakespeare's own from the stage (from 1674–1744).

Secondly, there is deep **dramatic irony** in the fact that physical symptoms of her guilt include the forlorn hope of washing clean her hands. We need to link this to both her statement that 'A little water clears us of this deed' (II.2.67) and Macbeth's insight upon actually committing the murder that 'Will all great Neptune's ocean wash this blood / Clean from my hand? No' (II.2.60–1). Although they share a common aim (to gain the throne), their beliefs are different: ultimately, however, all their beliefs are proved hollow.

The language of breakdown

It is worth noting that most of the play is written in **blank verse**. Notable exceptions are the Porter's scene (Act II Scene 3) and this appearance of Lady Macbeth. Before, and particularly in the first two Acts, Lady Macbeth's speech had been blazing and fiery blank verse – the strong rhythms reflecting her strong grasp on reality, and her determination. Now, she speaks in prose – choppy, abrupt, lurching from one incident to another, and even descending to **doggerel** with the rhyme of 'Fife' and 'wife' (line 41).

Shakespeare's writing here is brilliantly recreating what it means to 'break down' – the language is 'breaking' down under the strain she is under. It is therefore not surprising that she commits suicide – she can no longer hold 'it' together, and on death, of course, language disappears altogether. Note the contrast between the English court where the king heals 'Evil', and here where the disease is beyond any physician's competence.

SCENE 2 – Macbeth's enemies prepare to fight

1 **The Scottish rebel powers plan to meet their English allies at Birnan Wood.**

Knowing that Malcolm is marching north with a troop of English soldiers, we are introduced to the rebel Scottish powers who are determined to overthrow Macbeth. They plan to meet up with the English at Birnan Wood. The thanes comment on how uneasy Macbeth must now feel, as his inadequacies and guilt must face the test – and they are confident of victory.

From the imminence of action at the close of Act IV, we now find the hurly-burly of war – plans, preparations and advances. This scene helps accelerate the build-up – we are anxious for the climax.

The fact that the recovery of the crown by Malcolm is not solely through English forces is also important (bearing in mind that James the First was an audience for the play). Scotland, too, played an important role in casting off its tyrannical yoke.

Notice the imagery of clothing surfacing once more (lines 20–2) – Macbeth is simply not big enough to hold onto the crown: 'Now does he feel his title / Hang loose about him like a giant's robe / Upon a dwarfish thief'.

> **CHECKPOINT 17**
>
> What purpose does the mention of Birnan Wood and Dunsinane serve?

SCENE 3 – Macbeth is not afraid

1 **Macbeth is confident of victory.**

2 **He asks about his wife but dismisses medical advice.**

Macbeth enters with the doctor and attendants. He is in robust and fearless mood: the prophecies give him complete confidence that he is unassailable. A servant is abused as he reports that the English troops are arriving. Macbeth orders his armour and asks the doctor to cure his wife. He curtly dismisses the doctor's medical advice and enquires

CHECK THE BOOK

Shakespeare's Insults – Educating your Wit (1991) by Wayne Hill & Cynthia Ottchen is a wonderful compendium of Shakespeare's insults, including those in *Macbeth*.

DID YOU KNOW?

William Davenant's version of 'The devil damn thee black, thou cream-fac'd loon: / Where gott'st thou that goose look?' (V.3.11–2) was: 'Now Friend, what means thy change of countenance?' Which do you prefer?

of him, what would cure his country. But he is scarcely listening to the doctor's reply – his mind is obsessed with the prophecies, which alone guarantee his security.

The presence of the doctor again from Act V Scene 1 provides a neat sense of continuity and also of **dramatic irony**: the question of ministering to Lady Macbeth extends to the wider issue of ministering to the country, which has, as Macbeth notes, a 'disease' (line 51). Yet despite that, there is a part of him which still evokes compassion: his recognition of the life he might have had – which included honour, love and troops of friends (lines 24–5) – cannot but touch the heart. He knows, and relishes, what is good – but has chosen the opposite. This is his **tragedy**.

> **Macbeth's disease**
>
> The political aspect of treachery is never very far away. The comments on Lady Macbeth's health, mostly made by Macbeth to the doctor, apply equally to Macbeth himself. But he, of course, will have 'none of it' (line 48). Instead his restless energy seeks violent outlet – the casual way he orders the hanging of anyone talking of fear (line 36) shows how callous and depraved he has become.

That Macbeth is doomed should be obvious from this scene alone: the dependence he now has on the prophecies is paralysing his own decision-making and capacity for action. 'Bring me no more reports' (line 1) is a desperate statement for someone engaged in a war to utter – intelligence gathering is of primary importance. He begins and ends the scene reciting the prophecies – they have become a mantra to him. On them and them alone his survival depends.

SCENE 4 – Birnam wood moves

1. **Malcolm orders the boughs of Birnan Wood to be cut down and used as cover.**
2. **Malcolm's army advances on Dunsinane.**

Malcolm orders each of his men to cut down a bough from Birnan Wood and to carry it in front of them as they march in order to conceal their numbers from Macbeth. Again we are reminded of prophecy in the reference to the Wood. The witches only appear in four scenes (and two of these extremely briefly), but their influence pervades the whole play.

They learn that Macbeth intends to remain in Dunsinane – his strategy being to endure a siege. This is his only hope, since his troops are demoralised and fight for him out of necessity, not commitment.

A neat pattern emerges, which simply and effectively increases tension. Scene 1 led us into the diseased mind of Lady Macbeth; in Scene 2 we switched to the preparation of the Scottish Thanes who were planning to attack Macbeth. Scene 3 returned us to the castle. This time we witnessed Macbeth's diseased mind, but were also made

CHECK THE BOOK

Tales from Shakespeare by Marion Williams (1998) includes *Macbeth*. This is a modern retelling with excellent illustrations and some quotations from the play.

EXAMINER'S SECRET

Examiners read everything written down even if you have crossed it out – do not cross out something worth extra marks!

much more aware of Scotland's disease. Now, in Scene 4, we alternate back to the cure for all these diseases: the English army led by Malcolm, the rightful king. As Seyward concludes: 'certain issues strokes must arbitrate' (line 20) – a bloody operation to remove the disease by lopping it off. We have seen, therefore, the situation in both camps – and we note the contrasts. Now the battle must commence.

SCENE 5 – Lady Macbeth dies

① **Lady Macbeth commits suicide.**

② **Macbeth is informed Birnan Wood is moving towards him.**

③ **Macbeth orders an attack on Malcolm's army.**

Macbeth enters boasting his castle can easily endure a siege: he is confident of victory. The confidence of Macbeth in his strategy – bolstered by the witches' prophecy – is in marked contrast to the humility present in Malcolm's camp. He regrets that he cannot go out to face the traitors – too many have defected from his banner. A woman's scream is heard and Seyton goes to investigate. Macbeth reflects that nothing terrifies him now. Seyton returns and informs Macbeth his wife has died. For him this is a confirmation that life is meaningless. A messenger arrives and informs him that Birnan Wood indeed moves towards Dunsinane Castle. Outraged, and in some considerable doubt about his destiny and the meaning of the prophecies, he immediately changes his strategy and orders an attack.

Lady Macbeth's death was inevitable from all the comments made in Act V. But there was no point in showing it onstage – it is much more effective (and neatly symmetrical when we consider Lady Macduff's end) to hear her final scream. The interest of her death is in Macbeth's reaction to it. This can be read in a number of ways.

DID YOU KNOW?

Suicide is bad for you. One statistic found that 99% of young people who have tried to kill themselves, but failed, were a year later glad they'd failed.

- Is he entirely indifferent and emotionless – 'Signifying nothing' (line 28)?

- Does his **soliloquy** suggest mere cynicism as a last response – 'Told by an idiot' (line 27)?

- Or does the word 'hereafter' (line 17) signify his realisation of the real loss in his life?

Whichever might be true, and they are not exclusive, there is something in this isolation that he is suffering that cannot help but move us to pity him, despite our revulsion for all that Macbeth stands for.

Notice Macbeth's state of mind: 'I 'gin to be aweary of the sun' (line 49) – he no longer cares whether he lives or dies.

CHECKPOINT 18

How do the prophecies literally destroy Macbeth?

SCENE 6 – The death of Macbeth

1 **Macbeth kills Young Seyward in battle.**
2 **Macduff defeats and kills Macbeth in combat.**
3 **The battle is won by Malcolm's army.**
4 **Malcolm is acclaimed king.**

Malcolm, Macduff and Seyward with their army under camouflage approach Macbeth's castle. Battle commences. Macbeth is trapped but unbeaten. He encounters Young Seyward and kills him in combat.

Meanwhile, Macduff seeks out Macbeth alone. Macbeth's army capitulates and Seyward invites Malcolm to take the castle. Macbeth sees the day is lost but will not contemplate suicide. At this point he encounters Macduff. Initially, he refuses to fight Macduff, but Macduff insists. As they fight Macbeth mocks Macduff – no man born of a woman can defeat him. However, his confidence entirely evaporates when Macduff informs him that he was not 'born' (line 52), but delivered through a Caesarean operation. Macbeth is suddenly afraid and refuses to fight. He realises how profoundly the prophecies have betrayed him. Macduff now baits Macbeth. In a final act of courage Macbeth fights Macduff and is slain. The battle has been won by Malcolm and he now is anxious to account for all his friends. Seyward – through Ross – discovers his son is dead. As they commiserate on this, Macduff arrives with the decapitated head of

GLOSSARY

certain issues strokes must arbitrate only fighting can decide the outcome of certain things

Scene 6 continued

6 EXAMINER'S SECRET

Use other people's work for ideas and facts – but make sure you write in your own voice with your own interpretation.

Macbeth, and hails Malcolm King of Scotland. Malcolm gives thanks by promoting the thanes to new-formed earls. He intends to put right the evil caused by Macbeth and invites everyone to his coronation at Scone.

This scene is, in some editions of the play, divided up into four separate scenes. For the purposes of this study, this is not important.

Young Seyward is not a significant character in the play, but his killing by Macbeth is symptomatic of all the promise that Macbeth has blighted by his reign and activities. It also reminds us that Macbeth is, perhaps first and foremost, a warrior. The play establishes early on his ferocious credentials as a fighter – if we have forgotten about this, because subsequently Macbeth operates through murderers, then in this final scene we are reminded of where his true strength is. This is important – otherwise Macduff's achievement in slaying him in one-to-one combat is diminished.

The fact that Macbeth is primarily a warrior is also important in our final evaluation of him: through succumbing to the temptation that the witches afforded him, the witches succeeded in destroying almost every aspect of his true humanity. Even his courage temporarily deserts him (line 61) when he learns from Macduff how false the

CHECKPOINT 19

Why do you think Macbeth refuses to fight Macduff initially?

prophecies are – yet his courage returns: he will not yield. He will, as it were, take on Fate as well as Macduff – 'Yet I will try the last' (line 71) – and this, while it does not mitigate his crimes, does enable us to see some remnant of his great bravery.

Macbeth's analysis of the witches' – 'these juggling fiends' (line 58) – prophecies comes full circle: he was warned by Banquo (I.3.121–5) and now he has experienced and knows exactly what Banquo predicted. Further, juggling in a 'double sense' (line 59) ties in with the idea of equivocation running through the play. Equivocation, of course, particularly given its contemporary relevance to the Gunpowder Plot is synonymous with treason. **Ironically**, just as Macbeth betrayed Duncan, so the witches have betrayed Macbeth. When deliberating the pros and cons of treason and murder Macbeth commented 'we but teach / Bloody instructions, which, being taught, return / To plague the inventor' (I.7.8–10). This, too, has come true – he has had no rest as his own men and thanes have constantly defected from his cause, and of course his ultimate trust in the witches also proves misplaced.

EXAMINER'S SECRET

Always spend most time on questions that offer most marks.

The **imagery** and use of children runs through this play and adds a particular **pathos** to various scenes. Suffice to note here: it is the *Caesar*ean born Macduff who defeats Macbeth. Earlier, Macbeth had commented on feeling like Mark Antony before *Caesar* (III.1.56) when near Banquo. Clearly, Macduff is the man of destiny born, as it were, to destroy Macbeth.

The crowning of Malcolm concludes the play, but one important prophecy is still unfulfilled: that Banquo's issue will attain the throne. This means that the ending of the play can be interpreted in two quite different ways:

- It may be seen as a joyous occasion on which the innocent and honest Malcolm will make good all the wrongs during his reign.

- Some productions see the evil commenced by the witches as so endemic that another alternative is possible: namely, a cold and calculating King Malcolm surveys his victory – seeing Fleance in his army (not authorised by the text) – and realises that he must assassinate Fleance if he is to remain king.

Scene 6 continued

 DID YOU KNOW?

The themes of revenge and retribution feature strongly in Greek Tragedy.

Retribution

The final scene brings retribution on Macbeth. But as low as he has fallen, the final challenge from Macduff – again, challenging his manhood – does spur him on to fight. So, at least, Macbeth dies courageously. During the fight – when Macduff reveals his birth – Macbeth comes to realise how completely duped by the spirits he has been.

Now take a break!

Summaries

WHO SAYS ...?

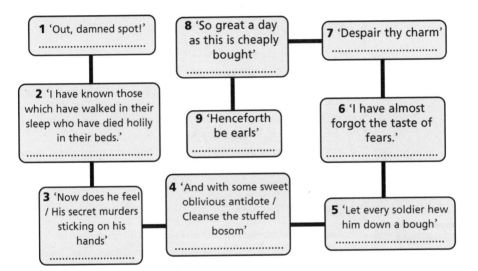

1 'Out, damned spot!'
....

2 'I have known those which have walked in their sleep who have died holily in their beds.'
....

3 'Now does he feel / His secret murders sticking on his hands'
....

4 'And with some sweet oblivious antidote / Cleanse the stuffed bosom'
....

5 'Let every soldier hew him down a bough'
....

6 'I have almost forgot the taste of fears.'
....

7 'Despair thy charm'
....

8 'So great a day as this is cheaply bought'
....

9 'Henceforth be earls'
....

ABOUT WHOM?

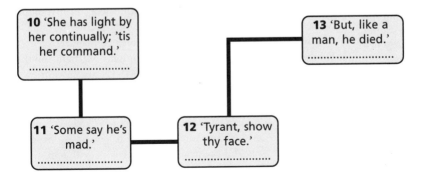

10 'She has light by her continually; 'tis her command.'
....

11 'Some say he's mad.'
....

12 'Tyrant, show thy face.'
....

13 'But, like a man, he died.'
....

Check your answers on p. 92-3.

PART THREE

COMMENTARY

THEMES

There are many themes in *Macbeth*, which is not surprising given the play's richness of language, character and incident. These themes include: goodness and evil, loyalty and love, hypocrisy and deception, justice and retribution, relationships, kingship, corruption, the supernatural. Many of these themes are connected – the supernatural, for example, provides ample opportunity to explore evil and deception, as well as to provide its own means of retribution. Central, however, to the whole conception and meaning of the play is the theme of ambition.

AMBITION

Ambition is the fundamental theme not only because it is the driving force of Macbeth's life, and so of all the other themes, but also it is the theme (in this play) which informs the Shakespearean idea of **tragedy**. In *Macbeth* we find that the hero's greatest weakness (causing Macbeth to fall from grace and inevitably die) is ambition.

Macbeth says this specifically when he is attempting to resist the murder of Duncan: 'I have no spur … but only / Vaulting ambition which o'erleaps itself' (I.7.25–7). This acknowledgement comes after he has considered all the good reasons for not murdering Duncan – only ambition is left to overrule his troubled conscience. Furthermore, whilst the influence of both Lady Macbeth and the witches is strong, their power over Macbeth is only possible because the ambition is already there. We see this with Lady Macbeth when she derides his intention to 'proceed no further in this business' (I.7.31). Her comment 'Was the hope drunk / Wherein you dressed yourself?' (I.7.35–6) clearly implies that he has raised her expectations of the throne – she did not have to raise the issue with him. And so too with the witches. Their intention is to meet with Macbeth (I.1.7), not Banquo. Banquo they know is incorruptible. On first meeting Macbeth we find him starting and seeming to fear something which sounds 'so fair' (I.3.51) and this can only be because his ambition has

CHECKPOINT 20

How do you understand tragedy?

 DID YOU KNOW?

The fall of the Earl of Essex during the reign of Elizabeth I happened only five years prior to *Macbeth* being written. Essex was perceived as being ambitious.

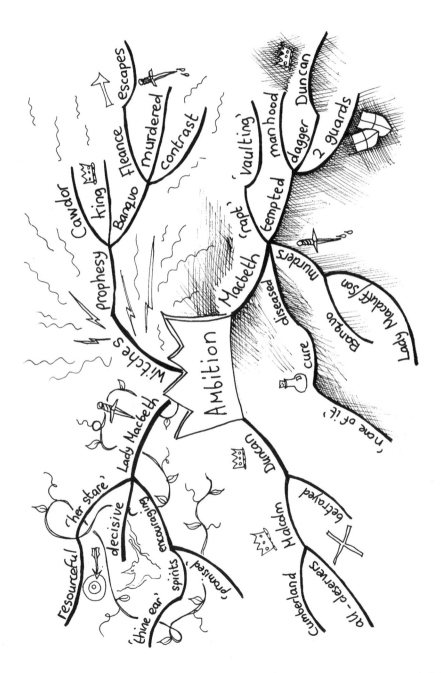

caused him already to entertain treasonous thoughts. Macbeth, then, is a hero but one who is fatally undermined by his ambition; and the consequences of such ambition – also explored through his wife who is similarly inclined – are the fabric of the play. Put another way: it is his ambition that leads the witches to Macbeth, and it is ambition which leads Macbeth to murder, treason, hypocrisy, corruption and deepest evil.

THE SUPERNATURAL

The supernatural, and witchcraft in particular, are also thematically important. Certainly, they are a major contributory factor to the play's enduring popularity. The presence of the supernatural in the play raises all sorts of questions concerning reality and appearances. Do witches really exist and have such powers? Or, more precisely, did Shakespeare believe in them? Further, assuming they did appear, was the dagger (Act II Scene 1) that led Macbeth on visible or an hallucination? And what about Banquo's ghost (Act III Scene 4)? And Lady Macbeth's spot (Act V Scene 1)? This last question indicates an area where the supernatural shades into the psychological, and there is much appreciative comment on how accurate Shakespeare's understanding of a guilt-laden conscience might be, although he was writing some three hundred or so years before psychology became a science.

Two points are vital. The first is to realise that in Shakespeare's time witchcraft was a substantial issue: James the First believed in witchcraft. People generally believed in it, and it was a capital offence to be a witch, because they were considered enemies to society. Thus, the witches are real, and any attempt to present the play purely in psychological terms does not match Shakespeare's conception.

This is important if we consider, for example, the invocation of Lady Macbeth to the dark forces (I.5.36–52): she is, in this scene, quite literally asking demonic spirits to possess her mind and body so that all human pity can be excised. To remove the supernatural aspect of this 'possession' is fundamentally to weaken both its dramatic impact and its grip on her being. The actress Sarah Siddons, generally considered one of the greatest Lady Macbeths, observed of the character that 'having impiously delivered herself up to the

DID YOU KNOW?

King James abhorred witchcraft. In 1592 he personally examined the witch, Agnes Sampson. He was astounded when she privately revealed to him the words he and his wife had spoken in bed together on the first night of their marriage. James 'swore by the living God that he believed all the devils in Hell could not have discovered the same'.

GLOSSARY

I have no spur … but only / Vaulting ambition which o'erleaps itself Only ambition spurs me on to make this great leap, which may prove to be too great

excitements of hell … [Lady Macbeth] is abandoned to the guidance of the demons she has invoked'. In short, 'naturalistic' interpretations fall short in their depiction.

Secondly, the supernatural is present in the play not *only* as an embodiment of evil. True, it is the witches we remember and their prophecies, because they are so dramatic. But set against these, there are references to prayer (II.2.24), sanctity (IV.3.109), cleansing (V.2.28) and even another sort of prophecy (IV.3.157). On this latter point it is worth bearing in mind that not only the witches' predictions come true: Duncan says, 'But signs of nobleness, like stars, shall shine / On all deservers' (I.4.42–3) and this occurs when Malcolm elevates the thanes to earls in the final speech of the play (V.6.101–3). But the most important aspect of insisting that there are two sides to the supernatural theme returns us to the play's focus and hero: Macbeth.

The supernatural backdrop to the play intensifies our sense of evil, surely; but it does not dictate events. Macbeth is a free agent and has free will. There is no **tragedy** at all without the realisation that Macbeth has chosen his course of action, and each subsequent action is a reaffirmation of that original, and bad, choice.

It is not without significance that the doctor's diagnosis of Lady Macbeth (applicable to Macbeth himself) talks of the need for a 'divine' (V.1.70). Even at this stage, confession and repentance are possible – although, as we know, not chosen. When the doctor mentions the requirement for the patient to 'minister to himself' (V.3.46), suggesting a need for self-examination, Macbeth's retort is unambiguous: 'I'll none of it' (V.3.47). One consequence of this, therefore, is that on the one hand, the supernatural is less important, perhaps, than its dramatic impact portends; but on the other hand, whilst mankind is free to make decisions, the presence of the supernatural does invoke a cosmic dimension and importance to all such decisions – this means damnation has a fearful reality about it. And, as we read or see the play, who cannot but think Macbeth is just such a one as has chosen damnation?

DID YOU KNOW?

Themes are major ideas which are explored in a piece of writing.

CHECK THE BOOK

Witchcraft by Pennethorne Hughes (1975) provides an excellent introduction to this topic.

STRUCTURE

EXAMINER'S SECRET

One very effective way to start work on your essay is to precede the essay plan with a Concept Map. The title or key word goes in the centre of the page, and then as related points occur they are developed out from the centre.

Macbeth is Shakespeare's shortest tragedy. One reason for this is that there is no subplot. All the action contributes to the central focus on Macbeth himself. This creates – as befits the intensity of evil in the play – a unified and powerful effect. The play itself comprises the traditional five Acts, which are then subdivided into scenes, but within that framework the structure is two-fold: we see the rise of Macbeth to power, and we see the fall. Both activities are prefaced by the witches' contributions. The turning point is in Act III at the banquet scene. Here Macbeth has achieved the full limit and splendour of the power he has and is ever going to achieve: at this point, Macduff excepted, the Thanes of Scotland are disposed to accept him. But the murder of Banquo produces catastrophic consequences, including the immediate usurpation of his chair by the ghost. It is following this event that Macbeth decides to revisit the witches, and from here onwards his decline in actual power – although not in depravity, which increases – begins.

This two-fold structure can be viewed in a number of other ways. It reflects the idea of crime and consequence: Macbeth himself comments on the dangers of 'even-handed justice' (I.7.10) and this proves true in terms of the play's structure: what he does in the first half of the play returns to haunt him in the second half. Equally, we see how the characters of Macbeth and Lady Macbeth pivot round the two-fold structure: it is Lady Macbeth who exults in evil till the middle point of the play, and her husband who is fearful of the damnable consequences; after the assassination of Banquo these positions are reversed.

This point about a two-fold structure should not surprise us when we reflect upon the elemental nature of the play: it is about good versus evil, and 'foul' being 'fair' (I.1.9). These oppositions and contrasts run through the whole play.

Now take a break!

CHARACTERS

There are many clues as to what a character is like in any work of fiction, but three questions are central to any full answer. What does the character do? What does the character say (and/or think)? What do other characters say about that character? If we bear these questions in mind when looking at the major and minor characters in *Macbeth*, we should form an accurate estimate of their qualities.

MACBETH

Macbeth is a man of action: the play concerns the things he does. He is a fearless warrior – and an important lord – who defends his king against treachery. However, ambition is his fatal weakness. He allows, first the witches' prophecy and then his wife's ambition for him, to undermine his integrity. It is clear that he is not easily won over to evil – his conscience is strong, and throws up many objections to his doing the deed. However, he is also too easily influenced in the direction that he secretly desires to go. Once he has decided, he does not deviate, and each step subsequently reaffirms his initial choice. Macbeth, then, is determined, and with his determination goes a violent and ruthless nature.

Ambitious
Courageous initially
Murderous
Imaginative
Hypocritical

One problem for him is that he has, initially at least, a conscience and a highly developed imaginative faculty – he sees all too well in his mind the horrors of what he is proposing to do – but he shuts out the implications of what this is telling him. He destroys his finer thoughts and feelings in his ascent to the throne. Many of these more sensitive aspects of his character are revealed through **soliloquys**. This leads to our view of him as a hypocrite: in public he behaves one way, but in private – on his own, with Lady Macbeth or with the witches – he behaves very differently. It also leads to his moments of weakness – before and after murdering Duncan, in seeing Banquo's ghost – when the strength of his 'realisation' threatens to 'unman' (III.4.72) him. The question of manhood is important in understanding the character of Macbeth. It is an appeal to his manhood that is Lady Macbeth's strategy in persuading him to murder Duncan in the first place; she also makes a similar appeal during the banquet scene.

And it is Macduff's final taunt that stirs Macbeth to fight to the death.

CHECKPOINT 21

How does Macbeth incite the murderers to kill Banquo?

DID YOU KNOW?

The witches are evil; God is good; Macbeth is human, and so a mixture of good and evil. This is what interests us about him.

Therefore, we can say that there is in Macbeth's character a profound need to prove himself, which he identifies with being 'manly'. Physically, Macbeth is strong; emotionally and spiritually he proves weak and corruptible. Ironically, by being corrupted, even Macbeth's courage is compromised – we see this not only in the final scene with Macduff, but at the moment when he succumbs to murdering Duncan. This was not only a treacherous act, but also a cowardly one.

This point about his manly nature is augmented by the comments made by Lady Macbeth. She thinks him 'too full o'the milk of human-kindness' (I.5.15) – an extraordinary statement in the light of the murders Macbeth commits. But we must remember: Macbeth develops and changes. When the play starts he is a god-like hero – a firm, strong, loyal character. But through allowing his ambition to suppress his good qualities, he becomes 'This tyrant' (IV.3.12 – Malcolm), this 'dwarfish thief' (V.2.22 – Angus) and this 'hellhound' (V.6.42 – Macduff). The character of Macbeth is a study of how one person can degenerate from 'Bellona's bridegroom' (I.2.56) to 'this dead butcher' (V.6.108).

LADY MACBETH

It might well be asked – so strong is the impression made by Lady Macbeth's character – why the play is not called the 'Tragedy of the Macbeths'? The reason is, possibly, that in her role she is not the co-equal of Macbeth in the way that, say, Cleopatra is of Antony in Shakespeare's *Antony and Cleopatra*. Her role is vital but also supplementary to the work of the witches: Macbeth is tempted to do evil and Lady Macbeth is the key human agent – the one Macbeth trusts and loves – who ensures his temptation is thorough and complete. Despite her initial overpowering presence, she is not, of course, a heroine herself. This is clearly shown by the way in which she collapses once Macbeth withdraws his confidence from her: she wants to support her husband, but she has no further role to play in his life. Thus, she withers on the sidelines and breaks down.

Dominant
Cunning
Determined
Haunted

Lady Macbeth, when we first encounter her, is dominant, determined, powerful, and even perhaps frightening in the intensity of her uncompromising desire for her husband to ascend the throne. We understand that Macbeth has 'deep desires', but this seems tame compared with Lady Macbeth's unquenchable aspirations: within forty lines of meeting her she is not encountering the supernatural on a journey home, rather she is summoning them into her body and soul! There is, then, a peculiarly imperious quality about her character. Further, we see in her actions – until her illness – a cool, self-possession. When Macbeth falters, she is there – and has the courage – to return the daggers, to faint at the news (and so distract attention from her husband), to dismiss the banquet.

The cast of her mind is practical – she plans the details of the murder – she has the future worked out. She is preeminently cunning. And it is she who has no truck with 'painting[s]' (III.4.60) of fear and supernatural solicitations: the dead are dead and cannot haunt the living. That is why she can say, 'A little water clears us of this deed' (II.2.67), because there is nothing to fear from God and old-fashioned ideas of retribution. This is also why she can happily envisage hypocrisy and falsehood. Her advice (I.5.60–74) on the subjects, Macbeth takes to heart and later returns to her as if it were his own advice (III.2.29–34).

However, like Macbeth, Lady Macbeth shows moments of humanity – she would have killed Duncan herself only he reminded her of her own father. It is these small details which perhaps indicate that she is not as cold and inhuman as she affects. And this of course makes her breakdown seem the more inevitable. Ultimately, water will not wash away the stain of blood. It is **ironical** that Macduff on first meeting Lady Macbeth refers to her as a 'gentle lady' (II.3.80) and one too sensitive to even hear the word 'murder' (II.3.83) – by the end of the play she is recognised for what she is, a 'fiend-like queen' (V.6.108).

Finally, it is important to note that Shakespeare seems to draw the characters of Macbeth and Lady Macbeth very much as a linked and complementary pair: when Macbeth is weak and vacillating, Lady Macbeth is strong and vibrant; when Macbeth is callous and determined, she is tormented and disintegrating. Their fates are inextricably joined, but her role and character support Macbeth's destiny; Macbeth, in the final analysis, is too preoccupied with his own role to give support to her.

DID YOU KNOW?

Lady Macbeth says she knows how tender it is to love the babe that milks her (I.7.5). This suggests she has had children. How many, we do not know. Or even whether any are living. Macbeth's obsession with his own succession suggests they are. Duncan, Banquo and Macduff all display affection for their children. We do not see this from the Macbeths.

DID YOU KNOW?

In real life we do know Lady Macbeth had one son by her first husband. This son was called Lulach – after Macbeth's death he claimed the kingship, but was ambushed and killed by Malcolm.

Generous
Regal
Honest
Trusting
Honourable

DID YOU KNOW?

The real Duncan (c.1001–39/40) was nearly the same age as Macbeth – they were first cousins. He was killed in battle by Macbeth, not murdered in his sleep.

Brave and loyal
Wise
Perceptive
Trusting

DUNCAN

Although he disappears at the end of Act I, Duncan is a major character. This is because his influence pervades the play, and in any case he sets the standard for what a king should be. Macbeth in comparison with Duncan falls so far short, although ironically Macbeth aspires to be a king like Duncan, for he admires him. Even after he has murdered him, Macbeth refers to Duncan as 'gracious' (III.1.65). And when Macduff argues with Malcolm, he appeals to the fact that his father 'Was a most sainted king' (IV.3.109). Therefore, the view of Duncan is consistent throughout the play (unlike views of the Macbeths) – all attest to his worth and merits.

Duncan is open, honest and sincere and perhaps the key word is honourable. He himself uses the word several times: first he uses it to describe the Captain (I.2.45) who has been wounded fighting for him – it suggests a combination of courage, loyalty and integrity. Treachery is the opposite of this. The openness and sincerity is shown in the free and frank way he praises 'all deservers' (I.4.43) and rewards them appropriately too. There is a warmth about Duncan – he seems to enjoy the achievements of others and his gifts are not given to gain his own advantage. It is awful to reflect that our final view of Duncan is his kissing (Act I Scene 6) his hostess, Lady Macbeth, to whom we subsequently learn he has sent a diamond by way of a present (Act II Scene 1).

He seems decisive as a king, and clearly inspires loyalty in his thanes. If he has a weakness it is a consequence of his goodness – his trust. He comments himself that it is impossible to see the mind's construction in the face (I.4.12–14), but this recognition does not cause him to behave, perhaps, with a little more circumspection: trusting Macbeth, he too readily steps into his castle without appropriate safeguards.

BANQUO

Banquo is an important character because he begins his place in the story running parallel with Macbeth: they are both worthy thanes, both great warriors, both loyal to the king. Most importantly, they both encounter the witches and their prophecies. It is the reaction to, and subsequent development of, these prophecies which provides the starkest contrasts between Macbeth and Banquo, and which is thematically essential to the exploration of the whole idea of evil, temptation, corruption and free will.

Banquo is courageous and loyal. And he possesses a wisdom and judgement borne out by events and acknowledged even by Macbeth, 'And to that dauntless temper of his mind / He hath a wisdom that doth guide his valour / To act in safety' (III.1.51–3). He notes Macbeth's reaction to the prophecies, spotting the 'fear'. He commands the witches to address him. Importantly, he sees precisely how dangerous such prophecies might be: how they might 'win us to our harm' (I.3.122). This foresight is amply fulfilled later. Perhaps even more importantly, though, in terms of his character, is the way he resists the temptation to do evil – whereas Macbeth is immediately tempted by the witches' words, Banquo resists them. And it is resistance that is the hallmark of his attitude to the prophecies – they seem to pursue him (since they cannot in his waking thoughts) into his sleep. But there, awoken, he exclaims, 'Merciful powers, / Restrain in me the cursèd thoughts that nature / Gives way to in repose' (II.1.7–9). Calling on heavenly powers to preserve him from evil is quite contrary to Macbeth asking the stars to go out in order to hide his intentions, or Lady Macbeth invoking demons. Banquo is a man of integrity – a man who has chosen to do good, and this whatever the cost. As he says to Macbeth, who sounds him out prior to the murder, he will 'keep / My bosom franchised and allegiance clear' (II.1.27–8). There can be no compromise of honour. It is interesting to note, in the context of his rejection of the supernatural revelations, Banquo is a keen lover of nature (I.6.3–9).

If there is a weakness in Banquo's character it might be located in his failure to act. Why does he not reveal what he knows about the prophecies immediately following the murder of Duncan, especially as he states that he stands against 'treasonous malice' (II.3.129)? That he suspects Macbeth is evident when he says – too late to alter Macbeth's coronation – 'Thou playedst most foully for't' (III.1.3). Failure to act on his suspicions costs him his life. And the failure to realise that – as the only other witness to the witches' prophecies – once Macbeth achieves the throne, his life is in danger is, perhaps, an indication that his 'wisdom' has a very definite limit. Like Duncan, Banquo appears too trusting.

Strong
Suspicious
Loyal
Forthright

DID YOU KNOW?

Costume, sound and props are vital. In Act I we find the following stage directions:

I.1 *Thunder*
I.2 *Alarum within*
I.3 *Drum within*
I.4 *Flourish*

These sounds and musical directions set the mood of the scenes:

Thunder suggests awe and mystery;

Drum suggests danger and warning;

Alarum suggests war and disorder;

Flourish suggests triumph and dignity.

MACDUFF

Fittingly, it is Macduff who discovers Duncan's murdered body, and becomes his avenger. He is a man of strong and emotional convictions. From the start he is suspicious of Macbeth – challenging his killing of the guards, and then abstaining from the coronation at Scone. Later he refuses to attend the banquet, and this leads to the murder of his family. Perhaps in this and in his flight to England we see two aspects of his character: we see what Malcolm calls 'this noble passion / Child of integrity' (IV.3.114–15) and alongside this the question of Macduff's judgement. Lady Macduff considers his flight cowardice; Malcolm initially finds it so difficult to accept that he treats Macduff with extreme suspicion. Was it the right thing to do? Perhaps we might argue that for Macduff the affairs of state were more important than family considerations, but this would be to suggest that he was calculating in some sort of political way. It seems more likely that Macduff is a character who is passionate for justice, and being swept along in the train of events – and his flight to England – simply did not foresee the extent of savagery that Macbeth would exercise on Macduff's family. However we interpret his flight, one thing is clear – his deep and passionate attachment and love for his family. His reaction to their deaths is one of the most moving scenes in the play. Haunted by their ghosts, he determines to kill Macbeth – and here too we see the compassion of the man who, in the heat of battle, disdains to strike 'wretched kerns' (V.6.27). They are not responsible – Macbeth is. With a sole and bloody purpose, equal to that of Macbeth's, Macduff confronts his enemy and proves his courage and his strength.

MALCOLM AND DONALBAIN

Once they flee after their father's death, we only meet Malcolm again. Their presence together, though, particularly praying as Macbeth is committing the murder, reinforces our sense of brotherly love and of a close knit family unit. Duncan isn't only a good king, but also a good family man. Malcolm emerges as similar to his father, although his harrowing experience escaping from Macbeth's clutches possibly makes him more astute: the testing of Macduff shows a desire to want to penetrate beyond the face to the mind's construction. But he is innocent in the sense of being inexperienced (so youthful) and also in the sense of being free from vice. However, he is dignified, determined, brave, recognises the worth of others, and can take advice. These qualities bode well for his future reign.

LADY MACDUFF

She appears in only one, yet highly affecting, scene. But we notice her anger, her wit and her courage. Her fate – and her husband not being present to protect her – must appear to her beyond all reason. There is in both the Lady Macduff and Malcolm with Donalbain scenes a sharp contrast when we reflect on Macbeth's 'family' scenes with his wife (and their content), and on the fact that it is the prophesied lack of an heir to the throne that so troubles Macbeth.

ROSS

Ross is mostly a messenger, albeit a highly ranked one – he informs Macbeth he is Thane of Cawdor; and he informs Macduff of his wife's murder. But through all these courtesies, one cannot help but feel that Ross believes in self help. He is at the banquet and requests Macbeth's 'royal company' (III.4.44), and although he warns Lady Macduff – 'dearest cuz' (IV.2.14) – he slips himself safely away.

LENNOX AND SEYWARD

Lennox is a courtier who suspects Macbeth early on, although he serves him initially. As and when he can, he switches sides to fight against Macbeth. Seyward is a fine soldier, who leads the English army. Shakespeare invests him with a convincing moment of **pathos** when he learns of the death of his son.

THE OLD MAN AND THE PORTER

The Old Man is a typical Shakespearean creation. He acts as a chorus or commentary on the action: his longevity gives him the right to comment on exactly how unnatural the proceedings have been. The fact that he is old is in itself natural – Macbeth cannot look for 'old age' (V.3.24). The Porter is a marvellous lowlife type of character – drunk, obscene, garrulous. The marvel is in how Shakespeare bends even the Porter's language to serve the themes of the play – whilst simultaneously giving Macbeth an opportunity to wash and change clothing before reappearing on stage.

DID YOU KNOW?

Shakespeare constructed his play from Holinshed's *Chronicles of England, Scotland, and Ireland* (1587). The book was three and a half million words long! Shakespeare freely adapted the stories when he needed to.

**CHECK
THE FILM**
Akira Kurisawa's
film, *The Throne of
Blood* (1957), is
based on *Macbeth*.
The setting is
sixteenth-century
Japan – the
deliberate use of
Japanese dramatic
forms creates an
alien and
frightening
experience.

THE WITCHES

We have already raised the question of whether the witches are
human at all, and if so whether they can be considered, therefore, to
have characters. There can be no definitive answer. Suffice to say, they
embody a malign and demonic intelligence. This, of necessity, is fixed
and elemental. Their information does tempt Macbeth – but it must
be remembered: they do not invite him to murder Duncan or even
suggest such a thing. Information is morally neutral until human
beings begin to interpret it. Thus they symbolise evil, but man is free
to resist them. Macbeth is tragic partly because he comes to depend
upon their information.

LANGUAGE AND STYLE

Macbeth is one of Shakespeare's mature tragedies – it was written at
the height of his powers. It is no surprise, therefore, to discover that
the language of the play is rich and varied. There are three forms
of language to consider: blank verse, prose and verse couplets.
Furthermore, comment needs to be made on imagery and symbolism
in the play.

BLANK VERSE

**DID YOU
KNOW?**
It is estimated that
Shakespeare had a
vocabulary of about
20,000 words.

Blank verse (sometimes called iambic pentameter) is the expressive
medium in which most of the play is written. Blank verse is poetry
that does not rhyme and usually has ten syllables per line. The
rhythm of the line comes from the fact that – usually – every second
syllable is emphasised, or 'stressed'.

To help you see this pattern look at the following extract:

> I will advise you where to plant yourselves;
> Acquaint you with the perfect spy o'the time,
> The moment on't; for't must be done to-night,
> And something from the palace; always thought
> That I require a clearness: and with him
> To leave no rubs nor botches in the work
> Fleance his son, that keeps him company,
> Whose absence is no less material to me

Than is his father's, must embrace the fate
Of that dark hour. Resolve yourselves apart:
I'll come to you anon. (III.1.128–38)

The syllables in the underlined words are 'stressed'. The pattern is clear – one 'unstressed' syllable followed by the one that is stressed. You need to repeat the lines loudly and slowly to yourself till you begin to hear the 'beat' or rhythm.

But notice, too, that if you extend the double underlining beyond the first four lines, some breaks in the pattern occur. For example, the line beginning, 'Fleance …' cannot follow the pattern because Fleance is pronounced with the emphasis on the first syllable: Fleance.

Notice that usually the most important words – nouns/names and verbs/actions – tend to get the emphasis – plant, spy, done, thought. This gives the key ideas greater prominence. In other words, the rhythm adds another layer of richness to the meanings of the words.

Blank verse can perform any number of functions:

- From a bald statement of fact:
  'The Queen, my lord, is dead' (V.5.16)

- To the skilful dialectic between Malcolm and Macduff:
  Macduff: 'I have lost my hopes.
  Malcolm: Perchance even there where I did find my doubts' (IV.3.124–5)

- From the impassioned soliloquy and invocation to demons:
  'Come, you Spirits / That tend on mortal thoughts, unsex me here' (I.5.38–9)

- To a weary resignation and despair of life:
  'Life's but a walking shadow; a poor player / That struts and frets his hour upon the stage, / And then is heard no more' (V.5.24–6)

Blank verse is flexible and its rhythms seem to reflect whatever mood Shakespeare is trying to capture in the character.

CHECKPOINT 22

The flexibility of blank verse is wonderfully demonstrated in Lady Macbeth's reply to her husband's question: 'If we should fail?' (I.7.60).

She says, 'We fail?' How many ways can this be said? Spoken flatly, it might suggest what will be will be. Equally, it might be said in tones of incredulity, or even anxiety. Which is right?

One way that Shakespeare achieves his effects is through his choice of **diction**. A good example of this would be: 'No, this my hand will rather / The multitudinous seas incarnadine, / Making the green one red' (II.2.61–3). Here the polysyllabic, Latin-like vocabulary of 'multitudinous' and 'incarnadine' contrasts starkly with the monosyllabic simplicity of 'green one red'. Macbeth's mind wrestles with the enormity of his crime – the inflated diction and its accompanying, sonorous rhythms reflects this enormity; and then switches to a direct and simple fact – for all the enormity of the sea, his bloody hand will turn it red. One listens to the effects; and one studies the choice of words.

PROSE

Prose is used in several scenes, most notably in the letter to Lady Macbeth (Act I Scene 5), the Porter scene (Act II Scene 3), the murder of Lady Macduff and her son (Act IV Scene 2) and the sleepwalking of Lady Macbeth (Act V Scene 1). In each case prose seems entirely appropriate for the task in hand. The letter to Lady Macbeth is concise yet interesting for what it omits to say. The Porter scene leads to the general observation that Shakespeare frequently used prose when dealing with characters of a lower social standing. **Blank verse** is more 'noble' or elevated and so for nobler characters. Thus, there almost seems a pattern in its use in Macbeth: namely, it does seem to indicate a falling away from nobility or perfection. Lady Macbeth reads the letter and immediately invokes demons and plans murder. Later, she speaks prose when she is mentally disorientated. Lady Macduff begins by speaking in blank verse but as the pressure on her increases prose takes over. She regains the power of blank verse – and so dignity – as she confronts the murderers. As for the Porter, his speech is quite overtly obscene as well as being an ordinary – but drunk – person's commentary on the 'hell' (II.3.2) of a place he is in.

VERSE COUPLETS

Verse **couplets** are used in two important ways. The witches use them in their conversation, and this is entirely appropriate as it suggests the world of spells and incantations.

CHECK THE FILM

A novel which attempts to portray Shakespeare's life using a richness of language to match Shakespeare's own is *Nothing Like the Sun* by Anthony Burgess (1964). For those interested in Shakespeare AND language this is well worth the read.

> Fillet of a fenny snake,
> In the cauldron boil and bake;
> Eye of newt, and toe of frog,
> Wool of bat, and tongue of dog,
> Adders fork, and blind-worms sting,
> Lizard's leg, and owlet's wing,
> For a charm of powerful trouble,
> Like a hell-broth, boil and bubble.   (IV.1.12–19)

Frequently, too, characters conclude a scene with a couplet. This indicates the end of the scene, but also, and often, points to a central idea. For example, the bell, for Duncan, rings heaven or hell: 'the bell invites me. / Hear it not, Duncan, for it is a knell / That summons thee to heaven or to hell' (II.1.62–4). The word 'hell' here – rhyming as it does – has extra resonance and depth. Macbeth's action not only produce a heaven or hell consequence for Duncan, it also rings Macbeth's own 'knell'.

WORDS

It is instructive to look at the language Shakespeare uses. Some literal words are constantly repeated to hammer home their importance to the meaning of the play. The repetition creates a dense texture. Words like 'done' (**ironically** the sense of being undone never far from such doings in the case of Macbeth), 'won', 'lost', 'fair', 'foul'.

If we take just one of these words, 'done', and see a few of its appearances we get some idea of how the word builds up.

- It first appears in Act I: 'When the hurly-burly's done, / When the battle's lost and won' (I.1.3–4)

- We next meet the word in the next scene. Ross says, 'I'll see it done' and Duncan replies, ending the scene (see **Verse Couplets**), 'What he hath lost, noble Macbeth hath won' (I.2.69–70).

- Later, Duncan asks, 'Is execution done on Cawdor?' (I.4.1) and by Scene 5 of the first Act Lady Macbeth is saying: 'That which cries, "Thus thou must do" if thou have it; / And that which rather thou dost fear to do / Than wishest should be undone' (I.5.21–4).

 DID YOU KNOW?

After the Bible, Shakespeare's language is the most quoted and influential in the English-speaking world. Many of his expressions have become proverbial. From *Macbeth* the very first line of the play is often used when three friends meet!

GLOSSARY

No, this my hand will rather / The multitudinous seas incarnadine, / Making the green one red my hand is more likely to make the rough, tumultuous green seas red

Doing and not-doing – simple ideas and words as they are – clearly relate mankind to his eternal destiny, as well as the outcomes of this life: winning and losing.

Other words, sometimes literal, sometimes figurative, become, through their associations, part of the rich imagery of the play: blood, dark, light, feasting, clothing and children. Because these words and ideas are constantly being explored and exploited, the net effect is to create a wealth of nuances and meanings, ambiguities and insights.

SYMBOLISM

The symbolism of the play is seamlessly connected with the imagery: blood, for example, operates on at least three levels – it is what is literally shed when wars and murders occur; it is also part of the imagery that pervades the play, creating a sense of menace and destruction; and it is a symbol for the evil that is associated with Macbeth. It is important in terms of the symbols to remember the Christian and Biblical context in which the play was written. Even Macbeth acknowledges heaven and hell, and the references to light and dark, nature and the unnatural, often allude to the great Christian symbols – the crucifixion, for example, is not only an event, but a symbolic one, and it has its parallels in *Macbeth*. We might like to think of Duncan as the innocent and good (Christ-like) king who is betrayed by one of his followers (or disciples), Macbeth. This, of course, parallels Judas Iscariot's betrayal of Christ. As you study the play, you may detect even more parallels – for example, the darkness surrounding the crucifixion, and the darkness on the night of the murder of Duncan.

**EXAMINER'S
SECRET**

In an examination there is no difference between being asked to argue and being asked to persuade!

Now take a break!

PART FOUR

RESOURCES

HOW TO USE QUOTATIONS

One of the secrets of success in writing essays is the way you use quotations. There are five basic principles:

1. Put inverted commas at the beginning and end of the quotation.
2. Write the quotation exactly as it appears in the original.
3. Do not use a quotation that repeats what you have just written.
4. Use the quotation so that it fits into your sentence.
5. Keep the quotation as short as possible.

Quotations should be used to develop the line of thought in your essays. Your comment should not duplicate what is in your quotation. For example:

> **Lady Macbeth tells us that she wants her husband to arrive speedily so that she can pour her spirits in his ear, 'Hie thee hither / That I may pour my spirits in thine ear' (I.5.24–5).**

Far more effective is to write:

> **Lady Macbeth tells her husband to arrive speedily so that 'I may pour my spirits in thine ear' (I.5.25).**

Always lay out the lines as they appear in the text. For example:

> **Lady Macbeth is immediately ambitious for her husband,**
> **'... and shalt be / What thou art promised' (I.5.13–14)**

or:

> **Lady Macbeth is immediately ambitious for her husband,**
> **'... and shalt be**
> **What thou art promised' (I.5.13–14)**

However, the most sophisticated way of using the writer's words is to embed them into your sentence:

CHECK THE BOOK
G. Wilson Knight's *The Wheel of Fire* (1972) contains an excellent essay, 'Macbeth and the Metaphysic of Evil'.

The fact that Lady Macbeth may 'read strange matters' (I.5.61) **in Macbeth's face shows how well she knows his character.**

When you use quotations in this way, you are demonstrating the ability to use text as evidence to support your ideas – not simply including words from the original to prove you have read it.

COURSEWORK ESSAY

Set aside an hour or so at the start of your work to plan what you have to do.

EXAMINER'S SECRET

In preparing to sit an examination it is vital that you prepare not only what you need to know, but also your mental attitude. You need to be:

- Relaxed
- Confident
- Focused
- Self-controlled
- Have high expectations for yourself

Self-controlled means: do not tell yourself things like 'I never do well in exams'. High expectations means you enter expecting a good result. To expect a bad result tends to produce self-fulfilling prophecies.

- List all the points you feel are needed to cover the task. Collect page references of information and quotations that will support what you have to say. A helpful tool is the highlighter pen: this saves painstaking copying and enables you to target precisely what you want to use.

- Focus on what you consider to be the main points of the essay. Try to sum up your argument in a single sentence, which could be the closing sentence of your essay. Depending on the essay title, it could be a statement about a character: Macbeth, despite the evil he commits, is nevertheless a courageous soldier; an opinion about setting: Macbeth's decision to leave the security of his castle because the wood has moved is a fatal irony; or a judgement on a theme: I think that the main theme of *Macbeth* is ambition because it is this vice, more than any other, that leads Macbeth to violate his own conscience and so set in motion the whole deadly series of events.

- Make a short essay plan. Use the first paragraph to introduce the argument you wish to make. In the following paragraphs develop this argument with details, examples and other possible points of view. Sum up your argument in the last paragraph. Check you have answered the question.

- Write the essay, remembering all the time the central point you are making.

- On completion, go back over what you have written to eliminate careless errors and improve expression. Read it aloud to yourself, or, if you are feeling more confident, to relative or friend.

If you can, try to type you essay, using a word processor. This will allow you to correct and improve your writing without spoiling its appearance.

SITTING THE EXAMINATION

Examination papers are carefully designed to give you the opportunity to do your best. Follow these handy hints for exam success:

BEFORE YOU START

- Make sure you know the subject of the examination so that you are properly prepared and equipped.

- You need to be comfortable and free from distractions. Inform the invigilator if anything is off-putting, e.g. a shaky desk.

- Read the instructions, or rubric, on the front of the examination paper. You should know by now what you have to do but check to reassure yourself.

- Observe the time allocation – and follow it carefully. If they recommend 60 minutes for Question 1 and 30 minutes for Question 2, it is because Question 1 carries twice as many marks.

- Consider the mark allocation. You should write a longer response for 4 marks than for 2 marks.

WRITING YOUR RESPONSES

- Use the questions to structure your response, e.g. question: 'The endings of X's poems are always particularly significant. Explain their importance with reference to two poems.' The first part of your answer will describe the ending of the first poem; the second part will look at the ending of the second poem; the third part will be an explanation of the significance of the two endings.

- Write a brief draft outline of your response.

- A typical 30-minute examination essay is probably between 400 and 600 words in length.

DID YOU KNOW?
One legend derived from the seventeenth century about Shakespeare was that he had been a 'schoolmaster ... in his younger years ... in the country'.

EXAMINER'S SECRET
Before the examination it is usually better to avoid mindless, nervous, and distracting chatter with other examinees. Instead, spend at least five minutes focusing on deep, relaxing breathing. This helps put you in the right frame of mind.

- Keep your writing legible and easy to read, using paragraphs to show the structure of your answers.

- Spend a couple of minutes afterwards quickly checking for obvious errors.

WHEN YOU HAVE FINISHED

- Don't be downhearted – if you found the examination difficult, it is probably because you really worked at the questions. Let's face it, they are not meant to be easy!

- Don't pay too much attention to what your friends have to say about the paper. Everyone's experience is different and no two people ever give the same answers.

EXAMINER'S SECRET

Keep an eye on the clock as you go so that you do not run out of time.

IMPROVE YOUR GRADE

You have spent some time studying *Macbeth* and, with the help of these York Notes, you have a good understanding of the play. Coursework essays and examination questions give you an opportunity to show your knowledge – they are not meant to catch you out or make you look silly. By following some simple guidelines you will be able to write with confidence and easily improve your grade. The advice that comes next will help you answer examination questions but may also be useful with other types of writing about the play.

Your potential grades in any examination can be improved. Your paper is marked according to a marking scheme applied to all candidates and no examiner knows in advance your level of achievement. All candidates start with a blank answer booklet.

The commonest problem is a simple one: failure to answer the question. Do not begin writing until you know precisely what you want to say. Otherwise, it is far too easy to go off the point and start waffling. A good idea is to look back occasionally to the question and check that you are still answering it.

Keep an eye on the clock. You will probably have two hours to answer two questions. Each is worth the same number of marks, so divide your time equally between them. Avoid the temptation to write at length on your preferred question and submit a skimpy response to the second.

One final point concerns the length of your answers. Your answer booklet is considered to be more than enough for the very best students to obtain the very best marks. There should be no need for you to request extra sheets unless your handwriting is extraordinarily large. If you are asking for extra paper, the chances are that a fair part of what you are writing is unnecessary.

IMPROVING YOUR RESPONSE FROM A D TO A C

- Instead of writing, 'Macbeth is consumed by ambition', you would write, '**Once the witches have finished their prophecies, Macbeth is oblivious to everything else. Lost in thought at the prospect of his future kingship, he comments to himself, "Two truths are told, / As happy prologues to the swelling act / Of the imperial theme" (I.3.127–8). The imperial theme begins to take hold of his mind.'**

- Instead of putting in a number of quotations to show how intent he is on treachery, note that he says, 'Stars, hide your fires! / Let not light see my black and deep desires' (I.4.50–1) and contrast that with his recognition of Duncan's worthiness as king, 'Besides, this Duncan / Hath borne his faculties so meek, hath been / So clear in his great office, that his virtues / Will plead like angels' (I.7.16–8). Observe that the recognition of Duncan's merits makes Macbeth's treachery all the worse.

- Instead of noting that Ross describes Macbeth as 'Bellona's bridegroom' (I.2.55), you could comment that he uses personification to vividly bring out the superhuman fighting qualities of the man – he is wedded to the goddess of war.

IMPROVING YOUR RESPONSE FROM A C TO A B

- Instead of writing that Macbeth instantly falls in line with the witches' prophetic suggestions, you could note the various expressions that indicate his mind is in sympathy with theirs, e.g.

EXAMINER'S SECRET
Examiners never take marks away.

DID YOU KNOW?
Shakespeare seemed unconcerned with the preservation of his work. The First Folio edition of his plays appeared in 1623 – seven years after his death. His two editors were fellow actors, John Heming and Henry Condell. They said, 'We have but collected them, and done an office to the dead'.

his first words on stage are 'So foul and fair a day ...' (I.3.38), which recalls the witches' rhyme, 'Fair is foul, and foul is fair' (I.1.11).

- Instead of putting in a couple of quotations, use detail from the whole text that collectively creates a sense of Macbeth being fascinated by witchcraft, prophecy and the occult.

- Instead of commenting that the writer uses similes or metaphors, you could indicate that he uses a range of poetic techniques to create an effect and give examples. Be specific about the figure of speech and the effect it achieves. For example, **'When Macbeth says that "Life's but a walking shadow" (V.5.24) he uses a metaphor that vividly brings out all that life is now for him – certainly, there is movement ("walking"), but what moves is dark and insubstantial. Life is no longer real and solid – its content has been emptied. He is in every sense a hollow man.'**

IMPROVING YOUR RESPONSE FROM A B TO AN A

- Instead of just observing how the Macduff feels (for example, when he finds Duncan dead, or when Malcolm tests him, or when he hears his family has been slaughtered), you can show how you share his views and can empathise with his ideas.

- Instead of just using references to illustrate the nature of ambition, you now present a line of thought about the subject with quotations to secure your argument.

- Instead of observing the poetic techniques used by the poet, you start to analyse how the thoughts and feelings are enhanced by the poet's use of language. Lady Macbeth's use of language changes when she begins to break down: **'The imperious and dominating blank verse gives way to couplet doggerel – "The Thane of Fife had a wife" (V.1.40). The firm and masterful control has given way to nearly nonsense.'**

Focus carefully upon the question set and plan your argument. Select quotations that accurately and relevantly support the points you wish to make. Higher-grade answers are achieved when you give a personal response that develops a line of thought, showing understanding of the techniques used by the author to affect your response.

DID YOU KNOW?

Shakespeare wrote plays and poetry. He did not write essays. However, there are a very small number of people who subscribe to the view that the great essayist, Francis Bacon, was the real author of Shakespeare's works!

When you have finished writing, you have one final and vital task: check what you have written. This is probably the worst part of the examination and no one likes reading what they have written. You have been working under pressure for the best part of two hours and you have almost certainly made careless errors. Now is the chance to correct them and send your paper on its way into the examination system, having given it the best possible chance!

SAMPLE ESSAY PLAN

A typical essay question on *Macbeth* is followed by a sample essay plan in note form. This does not present the only answer to the question, merely one answer. Do not be afraid to include your own ideas and leave out some of the ones in this sample! Remember that quotations are essential to prove and illustrate the points you make.

Macbeth – tyrant or tragic hero? Discuss.

THE PLAN

It is vital in undertaking a question that one breaks it down into smaller units, and then tackles each unit systematically. Discussion of the above question suggests at least four areas that must be covered:

1. What distinctions can be made between a tyrant and a tragic hero?

2. Evidence to support *both* positions

3. Clear indications as to which points are the most significant

4. Reasons for your final opinion

Let us look at these four points in turn.

PART 1

In looking at distinctions between a tyrant and a tragic hero we need to define what *each* is. For example:

DID YOU KNOW?
Charles Hamilton wrote a book, *In Search of Shakespeare* (1985) in which he presents powerful arguments that Shakespeare himself was murdered! (By poison, by his own son-in-law, Thomas Quiney!)

CHECK THE BOOK

There are many excellent biographies of Shakespeare: *Shakespeare of London* by Marchette Chute (1949), *Shakespeare's Life and Stage* by S.H. Burton (1989), *William Shakespeare: A Life* by Garry O'Connor (1991).

Tyrant

- all-powerful, totalitarian
- ruthless
- cruel and arbitrary

- capricious
- unsympathetic
- lacking imagination

Tragic Hero

- courageous
- weak, having a weakness
- driven by other forces beyond his control
- sympathetic
- imaginative but trapped

PART 2

We now need to link *words* and *actions* to these distinctions. For example, 'all-powerful and totalitarian':

- *Words:* he says, 'I could with bare-faced power sweep him from my sight' (III.1.117), although he decides to have Banquo murdered instead
- *Actions:* the destruction of Macduff's family (Act IV Scene 2)

Similarly, we can take 'courageous' in order to establish a more favourable response to Macbeth's character. It is not necessary to alternate the points, as the list does. One can choose to discuss the words and actions relevant to tyrant in a block, and then do the same for tragic hero. The important thing is to be comfortable with the way one has decided to present the evidence.

PART 3

It is important to indicate the relative worth of the various points one is making. Courage, for example, is a very important point: when we initially meet Macbeth he is defined by his courage, and when we last see him it is his courage which is at stake; it is also the issue of his manhood – his courage – on which Lady Macbeth tempts and persuades him. Therefore any assessment of Macbeth must address this issue.

PART 4

The final point is linked to part 3. Tyrant or tragic hero partly depends on the relative weighting of the evidence. It may be that he is both. Be sure, however, to balance your evidence.

CONCLUSION

The key aspect of reaching a conclusion is to accept the evidence which seems to contradict your conclusion, but then to show why it is not so valid. A good example of this might be if one concluded that Macbeth were more tyrant than tragic hero. The courage he shows in facing Macduff in the final scene does, however, suggest a hero. Therefore, to counter this one might present alternative explanations: true, he faces Macduff but not because he is courageous – but because, perhaps, he was more frightened of public abuse, or perhaps he faced him not out of courage but out of that same dogged devotion to prophecy that he had previously shown – he had to die then because the witches had said so. These explanations may or may not be strained, but the general principle is clear:

- Look at all the evidence
- Weigh it up
- Decide which pieces of it are the most compelling and why the counter evidence is less so

When that is done, the conclusion is likely to be convincing.

FURTHER QUESTIONS

Make a plan as shown above and attempt these questions.

1 Choose a scene from *Macbeth* which you think is a turning point. Write about this scene bringing out its importance in the play as a whole.

2 Write about a major theme of the play *Macbeth*.

EXAMINER'S SECRET

Ultimately, to become fluent in writing about Shakespeare, read the play often, see it on the stage and on video, say the lines aloud, and try to empathise with the characters. Ask, 'why are they doing this?'.

③ Write about the impact the character of Lady Macbeth has on the reader/audience.

④ Write about Shakespeare's use of imagery in *Macbeth* with particular reference to two or three major images.

EXAMINER'S SECRET

Examiners never take marks away.

⑤ Outline Macbeth's involvement with the witches. To what extent are they responsible for what happens in the play?

⑥ Compare and contrast the kingships of Duncan and Macbeth.

⑦ Write about the lives of Banquo and Macduff. Compare their attitudes and responses to Macbeth. Which of the two made the bigger mistake?

⑧ Choose two revealing scenes in the play, one for Macbeth and one for Lady Macbeth. Describe the two scenes in detail and explain how and why they reveal so much.

⑨ Compare and contrast the characters of Macbeth and his wife, Lady Macbeth. Which of the two has the stronger character?

⑩ Review Shakespeare's use of language in *Macbeth*. How effective is it? Give at least three specific examples.

LITERARY TERMS

blank verse unrhymed iambic pentameter: a line of five iambs

couplet a pair of rhymed lines of any metre – so Verse Couplet

dialectic logical disputation; investigation of truth by discussion

diction the choice of words in a work of fiction; the kind of vocabulary used

doggerel bad verse – ill-constructed, rough, clumsy versification

dramatic irony when the development of the plot allows the audience to possess more information about what is happening than some of the characters themselves have

epithet adjective or adjectival phrase which defines a special quality or attribute

figurative any form of expression which deviates from the plainest expression of meaning

iambic consisting of the iamb – which is the commonest metrical foot in English verse. It has two syllables, consisting of one weak stress followed by a strong stress, ti-tum

imagery its narrowest meaning is a word-picture. More commonly, imagery refers to figurative language in which words that refer to objects and qualities appeal to the senses and the feelings. Often imagery is expressed through metaphor

irony saying one thing when another is meant

metaphor a comparison in which one thing is said (or implied) to be another

motif some aspect of literature (a type of character, theme or image) which recurs frequently

pathos moments in a work of art which evoke strong feelings of pity and sorrow

pentameter in versification a line of five feet – often iambic

personifications a metaphor in which things or ideas are treated as if they were human beings, with human attributes and feelings

prose any language that is not made patterned by the regularity of metre

simile a comparison in which one thing is said to be 'like' or 'as' another

soliloquy a dramatic convention allowing a character to speak directly to the audience, as if thinking aloud their thoughts and feelings

symbol something which represents something else, e.g. a rose standing for beauty

tragedy basically, tragedy traces the career and downfall of an individual and shows in this downfall both the capacities and limitations of human life

CHECKPOINT 1
- By asking questions and riddles
- By referring to elemental forces
- By their appearance

CHECKPOINT 2 He is a man of consequence, courage, loyalty and some mystery too – the witches mention him. Why do they mention him, we ask?

CHECKPOINT 3 He does not know, as we do, that when Macbeth becomes Thane of Cawdor he will also be a traitor – and deceive him. Ironically, it is in becoming the Thane of Cawdor that Macbeth's ambition to become king grows.

CHECKPOINT 4 Macbeth's first words – 'So foul and fair a day I have not seen' (line 37) – echo the witches' words (I.1.9). This suggests he is already in tune with their way of thinking.

CHECKPOINT 5 Because they are saying exactly what he wants to hear and this can only be because they touch a nerve already present in Macbeth.

CHECKPOINT 6 If Macbeth is to be king, then this is something or someone he must overcome. It appears to trigger in Macbeth a deeper level of plotting and treason.

CHECKPOINT 7 This is a theme running through the play. Other examples include:
- Lady Macbeth greeting Duncan (I.6)
- Macbeth on learning of Duncan's murder (II.3)
- Macbeth inquiring about Banquo's ride (III.1)
- Macbeth at the banquet for Banquo (III.4)

CHECKPOINT 8 His openness is in admitting his feelings – which is in stark contrast to Macbeth, who flatly lies that he doesn't think about the witches.

CHECKPOINT 9 Macbeth is shattered and slightly hysterical. The deed preys on his mind – the more so because of the contrast with Duncan's two sons praying to God.

CHECKPOINT 10 To prevent discussion of what actually did happen that night. To prevent the guards denying their involvement in Duncan's murder.

CHECKPOINT 11 Vitally important, despite only appearing in a handful of scenes. Macbeth himself is aware of just how bad he is by contrast with Duncan. Duncan is a touchstone for true kingship and a measure of how a king should be. Set against his standard, Macbeth falls lamentably short.

CHECKPOINT 12 Up till then they may have been predisposed to accept Macbeth in the interests of peace, and simply to give him the benefit of the doubt. Now they know they must – and do – act.

CHECKPOINT 13 The sense of resistance to Macbeth's rule is now growing. From Lennox's words (and irony), we have Macduff's refusal to comply, and ultimately Malcolm's efforts in England to raise an army to claim back his throne.

CHECKPOINT 14 In leaving his wife and child unprotected, he might appear so. But it is likely that he could not have imagined that Macbeth would stoop so low as to kill women and children. Macduff was doing the right and brave and soldierly thing in going to join an army to fight Macbeth.

CHECKPOINT 15 He is testing Macduff's integrity because – with all the spies and traitors that Macbeth has created – he is fearful that Macduff might be on Macbeth's side.

CHECKPOINT 16 She understands clearly that Lady Macbeth has confessed to murder, and therefore to mention this would be to place her own life in danger.

CHECKPOINT 17 The scene serves in its reference to Birnan Wood and Dunsinane to remind us of the prophecies, and so tantalise us: how can Macbeth be defeated if the witches are always right in their predictions?

CHECKPOINT HINTS/ANSWERS

CHECKPOINT 18 Ironically, by his obsessive and literal belief in them. Believing the Wood to be moving, he succumbs to a fatalistic mentality and abandons his strategy – and the high security of the castle that would 'laugh a siege to scorn' (line 3). By foolishly doing so, despite the fact that on his own admission he has not enough troops to win, he ensures the prophecy comes true.

CHECKPOINT 19 Macbeth gives his initial reason for not wanting to fight with Macduff as – 'my soul is too much charged' (line 44). But is this his genuine reason, or is it his memory of the witches' prophecy: 'beware Macduff' (IV.1.70) – in other words, fear!

CHECKPOINT 20 Tragedy in the Shakespearean sense is not about some sad accident. It concerns a great person – the hero – who through some weakness of character falls from grace, endures intense sufferings (which fascinate the audience), and who inevitably must die because of the weakness.

CHECKPOINT 21 By appealing to them in terms of whether they are manly enough to do the deed – the same appeal Lady Macbeth made to him!

CHECKPOINT 22 Read the passage aloud to yourself several times before you decide how you think the line should be delivered!

TEST ANSWERS

TEST YOURSELF (ACT I)

1 The witches *(Scene 1)*

2 Duncan *(Scene 2)*

3 Macbeth *(Scene 3)*

4 Malcolm *(Scene 4)*

5 Lady Macbeth *(Scene 5)*

6 Banquo *(Scene 6)*

7 Macbeth *(Scene 7)*

8 Macdonwald *(Scene 2)*

9 Macbeth *(Scene 2)*

10 Macbeth *(Scene 4)*

11 Lady Macbeth *(Scene 6)*

TEST YOURSELF (ACT II)

1 Banquo *(Scene 1)*

2 Macbeth *(Scene 1)*

3 Lady Macbeth *(Scene 2)*

4 A voice Macbeth says he hears *(Scene 2)*

5 Lady Macbeth *(Scene 2)*

6 Macduff *(Scene 3)*

7 Macbeth *(Scene 3)*

8 Duncan *(Scene 2)*

9 Malcolm and Donalbain *(Scene 2)*

10 The grooms/guards of Duncan *(Scene 2)*

11 Lady Macbeth *(Scene 3)*

12 Donalbain *(Scene 3)*

13 Macbeth *(Scene 4)*

TEST YOURSELF (ACT III)

1 Banquo *(Scene 1)*

2 Macbeth *(Scene 1)*

3 First Murderer *(Scene 1)*

4 Macbeth *(Scene 2)*

5 Lady Macbeth *(Scene 2)*

6 Ross *(Scene 4)*

7 Macbeth *(Scene 4)*

8 Hecate *(Scene 5)*

9 Lennox *(Scene 6)*

10 Malcolm and Donalbain *(Scene 1)*

11 Banquo *(Scene 1)*

12 The murderers *(Scene 2)*

13 Macbeth *(Scene 2)*

14 Macduff *(Scene 4)*

15 Macbeth *(Scene 6)*

TEST YOURSELF (ACT IV)

1 First Witch *(Scene 1)*

2 Macbeth *(Scene 1)*

3 Lady Macduff *(Scene 2)*

4 Macduff *(Scene 3)*

5 Malcolm *(Scene 3)*

6 Macduff *(Scene 3)*

7 Malcolm *(Scene 3)*

8 The witches *(Scene 1)*

9 Macduff *(Scene 2)*

10 Macduff *(Scene 3)*

11 Malcolm *(Scene 3)*

12 Edward, King of England *(Scene 3)*

TEST YOURSELF (ACT V)

1 Lady Macbeth *(Scene 1)*

2 Doctor *(Scene 1)*

3 Angus *(Scene 2)*

TEST YOURSELF (ACT V continued)

4 Macbeth *(Scene 3)*

5 Malcolm *(Scene 4)*

6 Macbeth *(Scene 5)*

7 Macduff *(Scene 6)*

8 Seyward *(Scene 6)*

9 Malcolm *(Scene 6)*

10 Lady Macbeth *(Scene 1)*

11 Macbeth *(Scene 2)*

12 Macbeth *(Scene 6)*

13 Young Seyward *(Scene 6)*

Maya Angelou
I Know Why the Caged Bird Sings

Jane Austen
Pride and Prejudice

Alan Ayckbourn
Absent Friends

Elizabeth Barrett Browning
Selected Poems

Robert Bolt
A Man for All Seasons

Harold Brighouse
Hobson's Choice

Charlotte Brontë
Jane Eyre

Emily Brontë
Wuthering Heights

Shelagh Delaney
A Taste of Honey

Charles Dickens
David Copperfield
Great Expectations
Hard Times
Oliver Twist

Roddy Doyle
Paddy Clarke Ha Ha Ha

George Eliot
Silas Marner
The Mill on the Floss

Anne Frank
The Diary of a Young Girl

William Golding
Lord of the Flies

Oliver Goldsmith
She Stoops to Conquer

Willis Hall
The Long and the Short and the Tall

Thomas Hardy
Far from the Madding Crowd

The Mayor of Casterbridge
Tess of the d'Urbervilles
The Withered Arm and other Wessex Tales

L.P. Hartley
The Go-Between

Seamus Heaney
Selected Poems

Susan Hill
I'm the King of the Castle

Barry Hines
A Kestrel for a Knave

Louise Lawrence
Children of the Dust

Harper Lee
To Kill a Mockingbird

Laurie Lee
Cider with Rosie

Arthur Miller
The Crucible
A View from the Bridge

Robert O'Brien
Z for Zachariah

Frank O'Connor
My Oedipus Complex and Other Stories

George Orwell
Animal Farm

J.B. Priestley
An Inspector Calls
When We Are Married

Willy Russell
Educating Rita
Our Day Out

J.D. Salinger
The Catcher in the Rye

William Shakespeare
Henry IV Part 1
Henry V
Julius Caesar

Macbeth
The Merchant of Venice
A Midsummer Night's Dream
Much Ado About Nothing
Romeo and Juliet
The Tempest
Twelfth Night

George Bernard Shaw
Pygmalion

Mary Shelley
Frankenstein

R.C. Sherriff
Journey's End

Rukshana Smith
Salt on the snow

John Steinbeck
Of Mice and Men

Robert Louis Stevenson
Dr Jekyll and Mr Hyde

Jonathan Swift
Gulliver's Travels

Robert Swindells
Daz 4 Zoe

Mildred D. Taylor
Roll of Thunder, Hear My Cry

Mark Twain
Huckleberry Finn

James Watson
Talking in Whispers

Edith Wharton
Ethan Frome

William Wordsworth
Selected Poems

A Choice of Poets

Mystery Stories of the Nineteenth Century including The Signalman
Nineteenth Century Short Stories
Poetry of the First World War
Six Women Poetss

Margaret Atwood
Cat's Eye
The Handmaid's Tale

Jane Austen
Emma
Mansfield Park
Persuasion
Pride and Prejudice
Sense and Sensibility

Alan Bennett
Talking Heads

William Blake
Songs of Innocence and of Experience

Charlotte Brontë
Jane Eyre
Villette

Emily Brontë
Wuthering Heights

Angela Carter
Nights at the Circus

Geoffrey Chaucer
The Franklin's Prologue and Tale
The Miller's Prologue and Tale
The Prologue to the Canterbury Tales
The Wife of Bath's Prologue and Tale

Samuel Coleridge
Selected Poems

Joseph Conrad
Heart of Darkness

Daniel Defoe
Moll Flanders

Charles Dickens
Bleak House
Great Expectations
Hard Times

Emily Dickinson
Selected Poems

John Donne
Selected Poems

Carol Ann Duffy
Selected Poems

George Eliot
Middlemarch
The Mill on the Floss

T.S. Eliot
Selected Poems
The Waste Land

F. Scott Fitzgerald
The Great Gatsby

E.M. Forster
A Passage to India

Brian Friel
Translations

Thomas Hardy
Jude the Obscure
The Mayor of Casterbridge
The Return of the Native
Selected Poems
Tess of the d'Urbervilles

Seamus Heaney
Selected Poems from 'Opened Ground'

Nathaniel Hawthorne
The Scarlet Letter

Homer
The Iliad
The Odyssey

Aldous Huxley
Brave New World

Kazuo Ishiguro
The Remains of the Day

Ben Jonson
The Alchemist

James Joyce
Dubliners

John Keats
Selected Poems

Christopher Marlowe
Doctor Faustus
Edward II

Arthur Miller
Death of a Salesman

John Milton
Paradise Lost Books I & II

Toni Morrison
Beloved

George Orwell
Nineteen Eighty-Four

Sylvia Plath
Selected Poems

Alexander Pope
Rape of the Lock & Selected Poems

William Shakespeare
Antony and Cleopatra
As You Like It
Hamlet
Henry IV Part I
King Lear
Macbeth
Measure for Measure
The Merchant of Venice
A Midsummer Night's Dream
Much Ado About Nothing
Othello
Richard II
Richard III
Romeo and Juliet
The Taming of the Shrew
The Tempest
Twelfth Night
The Winter's Tale

George Bernard Shaw
Saint Joan

Mary Shelley
Frankenstein

Jonathan Swift
Gulliver's Travels and A Modest Proposal

Alfred Tennyson
Selected Poems

Virgil
The Aeneid

Alice Walker
The Color Purple

Oscar Wilde
The Importance of Being Earnest

Tennessee Williams
A Streetcar Named Desire

Jeanette Winterson
Oranges Are Not the Only Fruit

John Webster
The Duchess of Malfi

Virginia Woolf
To the Lighthouse

W.B. Yeats
Selected Poems

Metaphysical Poets

THE ULTIMATE WEB SITE FOR THE ULTIMATE LITERATURE GUIDES

At York Notes we believe in helping you achieve exam success. Log on to **www.yorknotes.com** and see how we have made revision even easier, with over 300 titles available to download twenty-four hours a day. The downloads have lots of additional features such as pop-up boxes providing instant glossary definitions, user-friendly links to every part of the guide, and scanned illustrations offering visual appeal. All you need to do is log on to **www.yorknotes.com** and download the books you need to help you achieve exam success.

KEY FEATURES:

Details on how York Notes can help you

Menu Bar to help you find your way around the site

Details on how to download York Notes

Quick Search facility to help you find the titles you need

Link to news about new titles

List of top-selling downloads

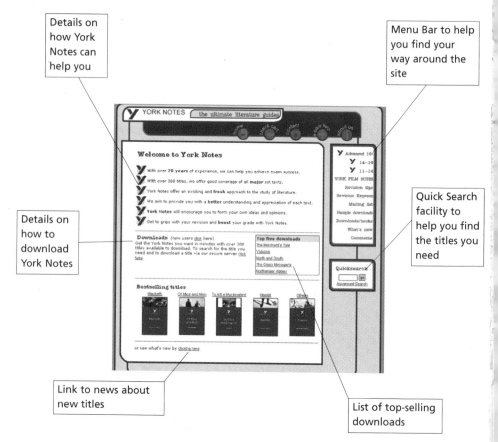